Brady G. Wilson is the co-founder of Juice Inc. Juice is an organization committed to creating environments where great results flow *and* it feels good to work. Such environments are particularly important for sales teams. Brady has unleashed profitable results for sales professionals in many of North America's Fortune 500 companies. His passion for creating breakthroughs for companies has spawned such innovative tools and programs as Pull Conversations™, The Five Drivers of Engagement™, and The Juice Check™. Also the author of *Juice: The Power of Conversation*, Brady lives in Guelph, Ontario.

Also by Brady G. Wilson

JUICE:
The Power of Conversation

FINDING
THE
STICKING
POINT

Increase Sales by Transforming
Customer Resistance into
Customer Engagement

BRADY G. WILSON

Published in 2009 by
BPS Books
Toronto, Canada
www.bpsbooks.com
A division of Bastian Publishing Services Ltd.

ISBN 978-0-9809231-9-3

Cataloguing in Publication Data available
from Library and Archives Canada.

Text and cover design: Tannice Goddard

Printed by Lightning Source, Tennessee. Lightning Source paper, as used
in this book, does not come from endangered old growth forests or
forests of exceptional conservation value. It is acid free, lignin free, and
meets all ANSI standards for archival-quality paper. The print-on-demand
process used to produce this book protects the environment by printing
only the number of copies that are purchased.

To my granddaughter Maya:

She susses out the buyer's hot buttons,
demonstrates great resilience,
and never fails to go for the close!

At under two years of age, she could teach us all
a thing or two about sales.

CONTENTS

Preface   xiii

Acknowledgments   xv

Introduction   1
The Sticking Point   2
Push, Give In, or Pull   3

The Sticking Point Process: *A Step-by-Step Preview*   5

Chapter 1
Pull Conversations: *In Sales, Relationships*   9
Make the Difference
Why Customers Buy   10
Push or Pull?   10
Pulling Works Better   12
Getting 50% More   12
The Payoff   15
What Are We Really Saying Here?   16
Put the Sticking Point to Work   16

Chapter 2

Why Do People Buy? *Welcome to the*   17
Feelings Economy

    "Soft Feelings" Drive Hard Results   19

    Why Customers Buy   19

    First and Last Impressions   20

    What Are We Really Saying Here?   21

    Put the Sticking Point to Work   21

Chapter 3

The Big Payoff: *Triggering Desirable*   22
Emotional Energizers

    The Emotional Energizers   22

    How to Deal with Your Customer's Energizers   24

    Six Advantages to Uncovering Emotional   25
      Energizers

    The Sale of a Lifetime   26

    What Are We Really Saying Here?   28

    Put the Sticking Point to Work   28

Chapter 4

Are You a Push or a Pull Salesperson?   29
Accessing the Genius of Pull Conversations

    The Problem with Push   30

    Why Most of Us Push   30

      Mental Muscle Memory   31

      Seven Reasons Why We Push as Salespeople   32

    Why Pull Works Better   33

    Logic and Passion Are Not Sufficient   36

    In Sales, Trust = Speed   36

    What Are We Really Saying Here?   39

    Put the Sticking Point to Work   39

Chapter 5

The Key Components of Pull: *Combining*   40
Inquiry and Directness

    Inquiry   40

    Directness   41

    Pull Matrix   43

    Blended Is Splendid: Inquiry *and* Directness 45

    How Inquiry and Directness Work Together   45

    "Other Than That"   47

    What Are We Really Saying Here?   48

    Put the Sticking Point to Work   48

Chapter 6

Step into Your Customer's World: 49
Understanding Their Reality

    One Salesperson's Transformation   49

    Relationship Tension and Task Tension   52

    A Tale of the Roses   54

    What Are We Really Saying Here?   58

    Put the Sticking Point to Work   58

Chapter 7

The Magic of Understanding: *Transforming*   59
Conflicts into Sales Opportunities

    Finding Common Ground   59

    Real Customer Appreciation   63

    What Are We Really Saying Here?   63

    Put the Sticking Point to Work   64

Chapter 8

Reflect the Customer's Reality: *Optimizing*   65
Your Sales Effectiveness

    Reflection   65

How to Listen Empathically 67
The Three Components of Empathic Listening 68
From Beginner to Master Reflector 69
Don't Walk in Their Shoes 69
What Are We Really Saying Here? 72
Put the Sticking Point to Work 72

Chapter 9
The Power of Invitational Language: *Welcoming* 73
Customers into Your World
  See, Feel, Change 73
  Invite Them into Your World 76
    Use Language That Lives 76
    Use Stories as a Springboard 77
    Use Stories to Frame Solutions 79
  What Are We Really Saying Here? 80
  Put the Sticking Point to Work 80

Chapter 10
The Power of Face-to-Face Conversations: 81
Speaking Your Truth Productively
  Be Direct 81
    Why Face-to-Face Conversations Release 82
      Energy
    Mirror Neurons 83
    Emotional Contagion 84
    Trust-Building Hormones 86
    Nonverbal Cues Are Meaning Makers 87
    Being Direct Earns Respect 88
    Ask the Unaskable 89
    Why We're Not Direct 90
  Speak Your Truth Productively 91
    What Is Your "truth"? 91

Use Non-Blaming Language 91
Examples of Non-Blaming XYZ Language 93
Use Humor to Take the Edge Off Your Message 94
What Are We Really Saying Here? 95
Put the Sticking Point to Work 95

Chapter 11
It's a Two-Way Street: *Checking Your* 96
Customer's Understanding
Help Them Reflect Back What They've Understood 96
Effective Ways to Prevent Misunderstandings 97
What Are We Really Saying Here? 99
Put the Sticking Point to Work 99

Chapter 12
Pull Out the Bigger Reality: *Performing* 100
the Magic of 1 + 1 = 5
What's Important to You? 101
How to bring Your Worlds Together to Find 103
Common Ground
Join Your Worlds Together with "And" 103
Ask, "What Is It We Both Want Here?" 105
Avoid "Dichotomy Thinking" 107
Draw Out the Assumptions That Obscure 109
the Bigger Reality
The Emotionally Intelligent Sales Rep 110
How You Get Triggered 112
The Amygdala Hijack 113
Focused Attention Increases Performance 115
What Are We Really Saying Here? 116
Put the Sticking Point to Work 117

Chapter 13

Pull Out People's Best Stuff: *Releasing Brilliance*   118
Through Respect

Respect   119

Respect Facilitates Learning   119

Person or Thing?   121

If They Don't Feel It, It's Not There   121

Respect Unlocks Your Customers'   123
Discretionary Effort

Are You Missing Out on Your Customers' Best   125
Stuff?

How to Show Respect   126

Caveat   128

Respect Is Person-Specific   128

Manage These Eight Deadly Distractions   129

What Are We Really Saying Here?   129

Put the Sticking Point to Work   130

Chapter 14

The Pull Conversation Sales Approach: 131
Engaging Your Customers

The Rehearsal   131

The Sales Call   135

The Debrief   136

The Follow-up   137

What Are We Really Saying Here?   138

Put the Sticking Point to Work   138

Conclusion

What Are We Really Saying in This Book?   139

Index   141

PREFACE

I wrote my first book, *Juice*, as a way of laying down the tracks of my belief that conversations are the "operating system" of successful organizations and individuals.

Writing that book has enabled me to write this book, which focuses on a particular kind of conversation: sales conversations — the kind you and I are involved in day in and day out, personally and professionally, as we sell and buy services, products, and ideas.

In some respects the message of the present book is similar to that of Malcolm Gladwell's *The Tipping Point*.

Gladwell's book shows how a service, product, or idea passes "suddenly" into public acceptance, often after time-consuming development and planning.

Similarly, *Finding the Sticking Point* reveals the role, in successful sales transactions, of patient, understanding, humane conversations. Specifically, it shows how sales conversations can find the customer's sticking point — the fear, the block, the objection that stands in the way of their "yes" — and answer it. This process aligns the customer's needs and the seller's goals — and results in a sale.

I would like to make two important qualifications about this book:

First, it is not a how-to book on the mechanics of openings, qualifying, closing, or asking for the sale. Rather, it offers an operating system — Pull Conversations — that will increase your success in executing any sales system you may use.

Second, it is not for sales professionals only. A broad range of people can benefit from it. We all sell at some point, whether it be a vacation preference to a spouse, a household chore to a teenager, or ourselves to a prospective employer.

The insights and the advice offered in this book have been of great help to my colleagues, customers, and friends in their homes and on the job.

My hope and expectation is that they will also be of help to you.

ACKNOWLEDGMENTS

I'm a grateful guy *and* I'm going to be brief.

I want to thank the entire Juice team for the way they build each book: pulling, refining, challenging, and encouraging until the final product emerges into the light of day.

I have profound respect for the intellect and talent of my editor and publisher, Don Bastian. He makes things easy.

I'm thankful to my family, who continue to express ongoing interest in my work and my writing.

And I'm thankful to God: an amazing person with a sales perspective I'd love to understand more.

INTRODUCTION

A Juice colleague and I were sitting in a restaurant in the funky Distillery District of Toronto with David Knechtel, then the leader of a cutting-edge training company called e-roleplay.

We were there to pick David's brain about our new business. We were quite unprepared for what actually happened.

David began to pepper us with a series of thoughtful questions about the nature of our business.

"What's your business model?" he asked. "Why do people buy from you? When they don't buy from you, what's the reason? What's your sales process? How are you marketing yourselves? What blocks you? What releases energy in you personally? What releases energy in your company?"

After responding to David's strategic inquiry for the better part of half an hour, we thought he would begin to dispense some advice. Instead, he just kept on pulling more and more information from us. Only when he felt he had a clear grasp of our reality did he share his thoughts. By that time, we were spellbound, taking in every word, every concept, every principle.

Why were we so open to him?

David had engaged us in a conversation in which we revealed our reality to each other.

A conversation in which we shared not only our dreams and successes but also our fears and obstacles. One in which our emotions were engaged and our energies released.

The Sticking Point

If you're in sales — and very few of us aren't in some way — your success depends on whether you can converse like David, reaching out and touching your customers' emotional needs.

Fortunately, you don't have to be a psychoanalyst or a mind reader to engage them in this way. You simply have to converse with them, searching for, and helping them with, their "sticking point."

A sticking point is what causes a customer to dig in and resist your approach. It can be cognitive ("This doesn't make sense") or emotional ("This doesn't feel right"). Although many salespeople dread the sticking point, it can be a thing of beauty. If you pay attention to it, it will lead you directly to what's most important to your customer.

Following the Sticking Point Process — which is summarized following this introduction and unpacked throughout the book — will help you identify and address your customers' sticking point. This happens through what I call Pull Conversations.

Push, Give In, or Pull

In my experience, salespeople act from one of three orientations when they run into a sticking point: they *push, give in,* or *pull.*

- Those who *push* their reality onto their customers trigger defensiveness. The result? Their customers dig in and shut down.

- Those who *give in* (acquiesce), fear what will happen if they speak their truth. They believe they are gaining their customers' respect by giving in. In fact, they are forfeiting that respect — leaving business on the table.

- Those who *pull* out their customers' reality generate the kind of understanding that creates trust, respect, and goodwill. Customers love working with salespeople who *listen hard and talk straight.*

Simply put, this book shows you how to find, and address, a customer's sticking point so you can transform their resistance into engagement — a.k.a., a sale.

THE STICKING POINT PROCESS

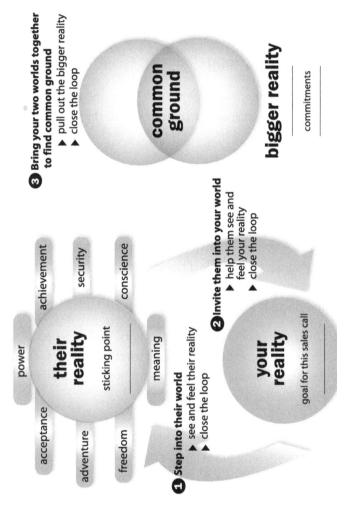

1 **Step into their world**
▲ see and feel their reality
▲ close the loop

their reality

power acceptance achievement adventure security freedom conscience meaning

sticking point

2 **Invite them into your world**
▲ help them see and feel your reality
▲ close the loop

your reality

goal for this sales call

3 **Bring your two worlds together to find common ground**
▲ pull out the bigger reality
▲ close the loop

common ground

bigger reality

commitments

THE STICKING POINT PROCESS
A Step-by-Step Preview

The diagram opposite and the commentary below describe the Sticking Point Process. You can use this process in two ways: as a rehearsal tool before a customer call and as a tracking tool after the call.

Here's a description of the process in point form:

- Start by stepping into your customer's world. Ask questions to determine what's most important to them. (Their objectives, their pain, their concerns, and their preferences.) As they respond, listen hard. Then close the loop by reflecting back to them, in your own words, the essence of their message.

- Once you've clearly understood what's most important to your customer, invite them into your world. Help them see and feel your reality. (Your goal for the call, how you can create value, how you can deliver relevant solutions.)

- At this point you will begin to detect your customer's sticking point:

  - "No time."
  - "No money."
  - "No need."

- Build trust and lower tension by acknowledging their sticking point and asking them, "What is it about _____ that's most important to you?" You will discover that the sticking point has a string attached to it. Pull it and it will lead you to your customer's core emotional energizers.

- Then bring your two worlds together. Identify the common ground between you: how your solution meets their core emotional needs. Frame your solution back to them so they can see those needs being met. Close the loop by ensuring that they've understood what you bring to the table. Say:

  "What would the implications be for you in your world if we could achieve this?"

  This will help them visualize the Bigger Reality: the solution that will give both of you what you want.

- Finally, summarize the commitments that both of you are making. Outline your expectations of each other.

The Sticking Point Process isn't meant to replace the method you follow — whether it's SPIN Selling, Solution Selling, Sandler Selling, or any other kind.

Rather, it is a powerful operating system that will:

- Energize you.

- Enable you to leverage the skills that you're already learning and using.

Chapter 1

PULL CONVERSATIONS
In Sales, Relationships Make the Difference

Here is perhaps the most important point that can be made about the process of selling:

The true nature of this business we are in is not about closing sales; it's about opening relationships: engaged relationships that will support many closed sales.

And what is the one *feeling* you need to create in your customers to trigger this kind of engagement? A feeling of trust. Very little money will exit your customer's wallet and enter yours without this crucial connection.

"Not so," you may be thinking. "As long as my product is superior to my competitor's product, it's not that big a deal whether or not I create a feeling of trust."

But in my experience, no product or service can compensate for lack of trust. In fact, we could define selling as *what you have to do when not enough trust exists in the relationship.*

Think of a customer who trusts you completely. A mere recommendation is often all it takes to get a sale. Now think of one who doesn't. A major campaign is required just to book a meeting.

Why Customers Buy

A pharmaceutical client of ours recently completed a study that revealed why their customers — doctors — buy from one drug company instead of another.

You'd expect that the doctors made their decisions rationally, based on the efficacy of the drug.

Guess again. The study showed that when the product of two drug companies was perceived as close to par, the doctors' number-one decision-making criterion was *their relationship with the account rep.*

You have to have a good product to be in the game. But success will be sparked by the trust-building talents of your sales approach more than by the superiority of your product.

And trust is built through Pull Conversations.

Push or Pull?

Every July I return to Manitoulin Island in Lake Huron to the cottage where I spent the summers of my youth.

It's not all fun and games up north. For example, a few years ago we had to replace the wiring between two of the cottages. Because the new wire was going to be buried, the job entailed running a thick electrical wire through a plastic hose that would protect it underground.

The challenge? How to get 140 feet of wire through 140 feet of plastic hose. Mike, the hardware store guy, had offered some advice, but it seemed far-fetched and time-consuming. My brother Tim and I decided to try something faster and easier.

First, we uncoiled the wire and stretched it out in a straight line along the beach. Then I tried pushing the wire through the hose. Although the wire was stiff, I reached a sticking point after pushing twenty feet of it through the hose. Friction was making the wire buckle in my hands.

We thought of taking the wire and the hose and hanging them over the edge of nearby East Bluff. Maybe gravity would overcome the friction and the wire would slowly fall through the hose. But that would mean rolling up the wire and the hose, driving it up to the bluff, unrolling it over the edge, sliding the wire through the hose (which we weren't sure would work), rolling the hose back up, and driving it back to the lake.

The hardware guy's method was beginning to look more and more attractive, despite the fact that it would require significant up-front work. We decided to give it a try.

Tim took a little piece of a plastic bag and tied a roll of fishing line onto it. I stuck the piece of plastic bag into one end of the hose, and Tim stuck a small vacuum cleaner over the other end. He turned the vacuum cleaner on, and presto! The suction pulled the fishing line through the hose to his end.

We then used the fishing line to pull a sturdy string through the hose. Once the string was through, we attached it to the electric wire. We were amazed that I was able to walk along the beach and pull the thick wire through the hose quickly and easily, with surprisingly little friction.

Pulling Works Better

When it comes to getting something flexible through a conduit, pulling works a lot better than pushing. Pulling reduces friction. It enables you to get something through in a shorter time and with much less stress.

When you run into a sticking point (resistance), do you become a push or a pull salesperson? (In fact, it's possible to enter a sales call where no sticking point exists and create one by pushing too much.)

When you need to get something across to your customer, your best bet is not to push what's most important to you but to pull out what's most important to them.

When they feel understood by you, they will be intrigued enough to reciprocate and pull from you. When that begins to happen, you can frame your message in a way that slides right through to them.

Here's an example of how this works.

Getting 50% More

"So, are we prepared to walk from this sale if the customer isn't willing to play ball?"

I remember putting this question to my business partner Alex Somos as we drove to meet Yorkton Inc. (not a real name), a prestigious organization that buys and sells companies.

Rob, the COO of the company, was planning to bring together the CEOs and General Managers of Yorkton's ten companies for an offsite leadership session. We were in the running to lead this session.

It was year one of our start-up business. Our cash flow really craved this sale.

We had met with Rob twice. We had done our research. We believed we had a solid solution that would serve his company. But Rob seemed to have a serious sticking point that was keeping him from saying yes.

This third sales call represented a crossroads for us. Would we be true to our values and lose the sale or sell out on our values and win the sale?

We hoped that a third alternative might heave into view: one that would give both Rob and us what we wanted.

But let me take you back to a key moment during our second sales call.

At that meeting we were trying to gain a clearer picture of what Rob wanted to achieve. We asked questions that allowed us to step into his world to discover what was most important to him.

Rob seemed preoccupied with what our approach was going to cost him. Alex thought he detected what was causing his anxiety, but we weren't prepared to address it at that point. We wrapped the meeting up and set a time when we could get back to him with our proposal.

Now, in this crucial third meeting, we started walking Rob through our proposal. Like most decision makers, he jumped to the last page. It looked as if he might use the number on the bottom line as a quick way to eliminate us.

Convinced that there was something deeper behind Rob's sticking point of cost, we invited him into our world and began to reflect back the implications of what he had said in our previous meeting.

"Rob," Alex said, "we think we're hearing, in what you've been telling us, that you don't want to experience any *unintended results* in the aftermath of this conference. Is that fair to say?"

"You got that right," Rob replied. "I've got strong, independent leaders of ten individual companies coming to this session. Our goal is to unify them better under our umbrella. If they resist some of the measures we want them to take, all hell could break loose. I'm concerned about losing money and time. And the whole thing could compromise my relationship with the CEO."

"We also want to avoid any unintended consequences," Alex said. "To do this, we need to meet with each of the participants. We need a clear picture of their relationship with Yorkton and their expectations for the upcoming offsite."

We definitely had Rob's attention.

"We feel strongly that this will be the best way to guarantee success for you, Yorkton, and all Yorkton's companies," Alex said. "In fact, we feel so strongly about this that if you decide against going this route, we will gladly give you the names of other suppliers who can do the work for you. Juice Inc., however, will decline involvement."

At the end of our conversation, Rob said, "I had a number in my mind when I entered this meeting. And the number you're asking for is a full 50% higher. But you guys have done such a good job of getting inside my head that I'm going to go with your approach — the whole thing."

The Payoff

Why do people make the decisions they do? Why was Rob willing to proceed with a solution that was 50% more expensive than he had anticipated?

We had discovered, hidden under his concerns about price, Rob's core emotional need for security: security in his relationship with his boss. When we proposed a solution that met Rob's need, the way was open for a sale.

Every time a salesperson encounters a sticking point, *energy is released.*

- If the sticking point is not addressed, this energy is applied to blocking the flow.

- If the sticking point is addressed, the energy is applied to creating a solution.

What's the payoff when a customer's sticking point is pulled out? It will lead you right to the customer's core emotional need. When this happens, a relationship of trust can be built, and trust will lead to the closing of a sale.

What Are We Really Saying Here?

- The true nature of this business we are in is not about *closing a sale*; it's about *opening a relationship*: an engaged relationship that will support many closed sales.

- People make their buying decisions based on the *emotional payoff* they believe they will derive from the purchase.

Put the Sticking Point to Work

In your next sales conversation, watch and listen for your customer's sticking point. If you're not sure you have identified it, ask for another meeting so you can take some time to reflect on what it may be. Then address it directly in your next meeting.

Chapter 2

WHY DO PEOPLE BUY?

Welcome to the Feelings Economy

Jim Letwin, the CEO of Jan Kelley Marketing, holds up a pack of Excel gum and asks his audience, "Why do people lay down a buck to buy this pack of Excel? What are they buying? Gum base? Soybean oil? Aspartame?"

People shake their heads.

"What *are* they buying, then?"

"Fresh breath," someone from the audience shouts out.

"Nope. What they're really buying is *social acceptance.*"

Jim makes a great point, one that marketers have known for quite some time:

People make their buying decisions based on the emotional payoff they believe they will derive from the purchase.

We are moved toward pleasurable emotions and away from unpleasant ones. In this sense, *emotions are what move us out into action.* In fact, that is what *emotion* means: *to move out.*

- When Ian buys insurance, he's not paying for a policy; he's paying for peace of mind.

- When Valerie buys a Volvo, she's not paying for an automobile; she's paying for a feeling of security.

- When Henry buys a Harley, he's not paying for a motorcycle; he's paying for a feeling of respect. (What other motorcycle will allow a fifty-five-year-old accountant to ride through town and turn heads?)

What's the key learning here?

Many sales professionals deal with customers on the level of fresh breath (the surface need: price, timing, features, and benefits). What's really driving the customer's decision-making behavior, however, is social acceptance (their core emotional need).

Tom Asacker highlights this truth in his article "Welcome to the Feelings Economy."* As he puts it:

> Your new imperative is to assess and appeal to your customers' feelings — period. Feelings are the basis for all profit-generating consumption in a market at the mercy of customer choice. Focus on feelings, especially the subtle ones that customers themselves cannot articulate.

In the story in the previous chapter, Rob's surface need — his sticking point — was cost. His core emotional need was

---

security: He didn't want any surprises, because that would undermine his security with his boss. If we had not pulled this out, we would have jeopardized his and his company's success and minimized our earning power.

"Soft Feelings" Drive Hard Results

What makes the sticking point sticky? Emotions.

You've probably had the experience where a perfectly rational customer becomes irrationally resistant to your approach.

People's emotional needs drive their decisions. In fact, their behaviors can best be understood as *an attempt to get their emotional needs met.* If this is true, the most important thing you can do as a sales professional is create an environment in which your customer's core emotional needs can be met.

This is when *pull* is so critical.

Why?

Because people's core emotional needs are invisible. We've yet to meet customers who have them tattooed on their forehead. And just to compound the issue, each and every customer is driven by *different* emotional needs.

Why Customers Buy

On the surface, it seems that customers buy based on logic: their assessment of things like quality, convenience, value, or a reputable brand. However, deeper reasons are driving their buying behavior.

Buying decisions are usually a blend of rational and emotional judgments. And which type of judgment do you suppose has the power to trump the other? You guessed it: emotional judgments. To quote Asacker again:

> In an oversupplied market with an incomprehensible amount of conflicting information, rational decision-making is a myth.

Whenever the customer's logic is in an argument with their gut, emotional judgments win the day. Why is this so?

First and Last Impressions

One reason has to do with first and last impressions.

Brain researchers have discovered that data entering the prefrontal cortex (the logical, decision-making center of the brain) are first filtered through the amygdala (the emotional center of the brain).

In short, we humans feel first, *then* we think. That means the first impression you make on your customer is an emotional one. Your customer is unconsciously asking herself during those first few seconds, "Can I connect with this person? Is he safe? Interesting? Off-putting?"

What's equally important is what happens long after your customer encounter has concluded. People can't always remember what you said or what you did, but they sure remember how you made them feel.

Do your customers feel listened to? Put down? Excited? Patronized?

What Are We Really Saying Here?

- A primary decision-making criterion for customers is how the account rep makes them feel.

- Emotional judgments win the day whenever the customer's logic is in an argument with their gut.

Put the Sticking Point to Work

- Review your last two or three successful sales. Were the customers' decisions made primarily on rational or emotional lines?

- Do the same for your last two or three unsuccessful sales.

Chapter 3

THE BIG PAYOFF

Triggering Desirable Emotional Energizers

We move away from people who trigger undesirable emotions.

We move toward people who trigger desirable emotions.

The question I've been wrestling with for years is this: What are the core emotions that drive a customer's decision-making behavior? Here's what I have learned.

The Emotional Energizers

I believe there are eight emotional drivers — what I also call *emotional energizers* — that drive buyers' decisions:

- A feeling of **power**: "This can die or this can fly. And I decide."

- A feeling of **achievement**: "This will get us great results."

- A feeling of **security**: "This will be a safe decision."

- A feeling of **conscience**: "This is just the right thing to do."

- A feeling of **meaning**: "This will make a difference."

- A feeling of **freedom**: "Doing this will free me up."

- A feeling of **adventure**: "This will be exciting."

- A feeling of **acceptance**: "I'll be more included if I do this."

Visualize these eight energizers in a circle.

You may have noticed that the energizers on opposing sides of the circle tend to be at odds with each other.

- A customer will make a choice based on conscience or a desire for acceptance. The two are often in tension.

- The customer who chooses security will likely forfeit adventure.

- The customer who is intent on meaning may have to give up power.

- The customer who wants maximum freedom may have to forfeit achievement.

You may have also noticed that the energizers next to each other tend to be somewhat related.

- Freedom is related to adventure and also to meaning.

- Power is related to acceptance and also to achievement.

How to Deal with Your Customer's Energizers

We have found that customers have at least three energizers that are most important to them. With a little attention, you will be able to detect what they are.

Even though on the surface it would appear that customers are buying one thing, there typically is a deeper reason for their buying behavior: *an emotional energizer that they refuse to do without*. Your job is to get beneath the surface need (fresh breath) and uncover the deeper need (social acceptance).

Remember, there's a string attached to each sticking point. Pull on it and it will lead you to a core emotional energizer.

- The customer with a sticking point of convenience may have an energizer of freedom: "I don't want to ever have to worry about this again."

- The customer with a sticking point of quality may have an energizer of security: "I don't want anybody coming after me telling me that this broke down."

- The customer with a sticking point of value may have an energizer of conscience: "It's my responsibility to be a good steward of my company's resources."

- The customer with a sticking point of excellence may have an energizer of achievement: "Our company deals with only the best."

"But isn't it enough to understand the surface need?" you may be wondering. "Why bother analyzing people like this?"

Six Advantages to Uncovering Emotional Energizers

1. You can craft a more intelligent solution. This ensures that your product/solution cannot be easily commoditized.

2. You can frame your offering in a way that custom fits your customer's deepest (unstated) needs.

3. You can charge a premium for what you sell.

4. You can more accurately interpret and even anticipate your customer's words and actions.

5. You can build a firewall around your customer. This makes it difficult for a competitor to dislodge you with lower prices.

6. You can achieve the amazing relationship of customer engagement. Customers will give you their discretionary effort and their goodwill. They will create opportunities for you, accommodate your needs, and even make sacrifices for you. You have entered into a respectful partnership.

The Sale of a Lifetime

Fred deVries, a medical equipment sales rep, made a stunning sale to a large hospital a few years ago. It would have been tragic if he hadn't. Fred had invested a year of his career, hundreds of hours of his time, and thousands and thousands of company dollars in the effort.

Since this was the largest sale in the history of his company, Fred was flown down to Texas to share his secrets with all the North American sales reps. Rather than playing the guru, however, he invited someone from the hospital to give her perspective on why he got the sale.

Here's what she told the reps:

Get to know your customer. Fred spent as much time as possible with us. He got to know each of our little wins, what scratched our itch, how often each of us wanted to see him. He invested in us without knowing if he would get the deal.

Fred went beyond the surface need and pulled out the core emotional need of his customers at every possible opportunity:

- He made it his business to understand what a "little win" was for each decision maker. This enabled him to make the most of his time and energy investments.

- He maintained a detailed profile sheet on each of the key players. This helped him to avoid making assumptions.

- He spent time with the nurses where they worked. This enabled him to understand the aspects of his company's instruments that would be most valuable to them.

- He sponsored nurses' trade shows. This demonstrated his support for them and their profession.

- He wrote down, remembered, and referred to the tiny "wouldn't it be nice" requests of the people he called on. This demonstrated that he understood what was important to them — what made them light up.

A combination of emotions creates the exciting voltage of customer engagement:

- The product is achieving great results.

- It's freeing people up and making them look great.

- The partnership is trust-filled and feels solid and strong.

- People feel attended to and respected.

In the final analysis, Fred produced this combination by understanding what drove the decision-making behavior of each of his customers. This yielded him the most dynamic result of his career: a $7.8-million sale and an $11.5-million year — 403% of his quota.

When you get to the deeper reasons inside an account, you set yourself up for multiples of success.

Do you know the emotional energizers of each of your key accounts? In the next chapter, we'll unpack the concept of Pull Conversation, a powerful way for you to uncover what is most important to your customers.

What Are We Really Saying Here?

- The key to making a sale is triggering desirable emotions in your customers — emotions that *they* desire.

- Your customers' main emotional energizers are the key to their purchases.

Put the Sticking Point to Work

Take a moment and reflect on one customer relationship that could be strengthened by uncovering that customer's emotional energizers. Write out at least one thing you might do differently.

Chapter 4

ARE YOU A PUSH OR A PULL SALESPERSON?

Accessing the Genius of Pull Conversations

W hen push is prevalent in our sales relationships and approaches, we overlook clues to what the customer's sticking point is.

As a result, we fail to meet core emotional needs.

And as a result of that, we miss the sale.

Think, for example, of a sales relationship that went off the rails for you: the one you wish you could do over. To what extent was *push* part of the problem?

You may be thinking, "But isn't there a time to *push*, to passionately advocate your own point of view?" Absolutely. When is that time? Once you have *pulled* first.

When pulling has proven to the customer that you are truly interested in *their* perspective, *their* needs, and *their* desires, they will want to understand what you have to offer.

In short, pulling earns you the right to advocate your point of view.

The Problem with Push

Picture yourself in a meeting with your sales team. You have a strong point of view about the topic being discussed. You believe your job is to push your point of view out to others until they get it.

As you begin to push, you trigger defensiveness in your teammates. You sense their resistance, so you push more. You have to get your point through to them.

They dig in even more and become less receptive to your ideas. Two team members outright stonewall you. Three or four others nod politely and say they will consider your point of view.

At this point, whether you know it or not, your idea is dead in the water.

Why Most of Us Push

Years ago I heard about a study the Jack Carew Organization conducted with 30,000 sales professionals. They discovered that in any sales interaction the odds are two to one that "the orientation of the salesperson is inwardly focused."

What does that look like? The customer makes a comment and the salesperson's mind goes immediately to, "What does that mean to my quota — to my ability to get this sale?" It doesn't go to, "What does that comment mean to this customer — to her key objectives, to her history with other vendors?"

Think of it. Only a third of the sales world is customer-centric.

Check it out for yourself. Look around your personal and professional worlds. Is this what you see? Your experience will probably bear the statistic out.

Being self-centered is a severe handicap when it comes to drawing out what's most important to the customer.

Imagine it otherwise. Imagine a world where salespeople use Pull Conversations to understand what's most important to their customers. Imagine the results your company could produce if every colleague on your sales team mastered this approach.

Let's look at the reasons why push is so instinctive to us and how we can develop a pull mindset.

Mental Muscle Memory

A good friend of mine, a police officer, tells me that police academies have had to change the way they train their officers to disarm an assailant.

Here's how they were teaching this technique. They had an assailant point a gun at an officer and the officer execute a swift technique of grabbing the firearm out of the assailant's hand. Then, in order to practice the move again, the officer handed the gun back to the assailant. The cycle was repeated until the technique could be completed flawlessly.

You probably know where this is going. There is tragic video footage of an off-duty officer encountering a robber. The robber points the gun at the officer and the officer smoothly extracts the gun from the robber's hand — and then hands it back. The robber then shoots the officer.

Mental muscle memory (MMM) is a powerful thing. Have you ever driven up to your house and wondered, "How did I get here? Did I go through any red lights? I can't even remember!"

How can this be? Because MMM takes care of 90% of your drive from work.

The problem with MMM is in how easily we can develop habits that make us ineffective. Are there ways in which you figuratively "hand the gun back" (do something out of sheer habit) and get an unintended negative result?

Many of us have a long history of pushing first in any sales conversation. We have created MMM that is difficult to recalibrate.

In fact, there are at least seven factors that strongly influence us to take a push-first approach.

Seven Reasons Why We Push as Salespeople

1. We operate from a powerful *assumption* that "there's no time to pull."

2. We experience *insecurity* and start spouting information.

3. We suffer from *hubris* (swollen ego). "I know what they need better than they do."

4. We don't want to be *perceived as a pushover or as unknowledgeable.*

5. Our *competitive sales culture* seems to demand it.

6. Our *quotas* drive us. "There's so much at stake here, I *have* to push."

7. We *lack modeling*. Who has ever showed you how to pull?

My guess is that the concept of pulling before you push is not rocket science to you. But can you identify the source of your resistance when you don't do this? Is your top reason for pushing instead of pulling included as one of the seven above? If not, feel free to add it to the list.

Ask yourself, when you're on your next sales call, "Why am I pushing right now?"

Police officer training is different now. After the assailant points the gun and the officer takes it away, he then points the gun at the assailant. That marks the end of the cycle. Officers practice this drill until they have fully recalibrated their MMM.

And that's the good news about MMM. Your neural pathways *can* be recalibrated. With practice, you can create MMM that will systematically trigger behaviors that are highly productive.

Let's examine exactly why Pull Conversations are a more effective way to sell.

Why Pull Works Better

Let's say the marketing team of Lexus executes a particularly successful ad campaign. Every ad creates a powerful feeling inside each different consumer group. And that feeling creates curiosity and interest. Consumer interest has a singular effect on the carmaker's sales force: It makes their jobs much easier. Sales increase.

What can you learn from the above approach to consumers? The marketing group didn't indiscriminately throw out a bunch of messages to a broad cross-section of consumers and hope something would stick. They strategically placed one Lexus ad in *Men's Fitness* magazine and a very different one in *Chatelaine*.

What makes marketers successful? The same thing that makes you successful as a salesperson: They pull.

1. First they step into the consumer's world and pull out the emotions that drive the buying decision.

2. Then they create a narrative that evokes a powerful feeling. This feeling pulls the consumer into their organization's world. It causes them to be interested in their organization's product.

There's a whole science and history behind pull.

In the 1950s, Toyota shifted manufacturing from a push to a pull mindset. They began to pull resources into the assembly line as needed, rather than stockpiling huge inventories of parts. It wasn't long before marketing organizations began to adopt the pull methodology.

The media have shifted to a pull approach within the past decade.

In several business sectors, people are discovering that pull works better than push.

When I'm running a training session, I ask participants, "What's the best way to make yourself understood? To push, pull, or give in?" Usually a full 95% respond, "Pull works best."

Then I say, "I believe you, but sell this to me. Why do you believe it works best?"

Here's what they say:

- *Pull* reduces the other person's defensiveness and increases respect and trust, making them receptive and willing to understand you.

- *Pull* enables you to understand the other person's sticking point: the place where they dig in their heels and resist your approach. It could be a cognitive sticking point ("This doesn't make sense") or an emotional sticking point ("This doesn't feel right"). Once you pull out their sticking point, you can frame your message in a way that's easy for them to understand and relate to.

- If there is a block, an error, or a response that is out of context, *pull* can show you what it is. Identifying this is the best chance you have to address the sticking point and re-establish a path for reaching common goals.

- *Pull* does a better job than push if you need the other person to embrace your expertise rather than just give cognitive assent to it. *Pull* helps a prospect buy into your approach.

- The solution may not be either yours or theirs but a hybrid of the two. If you *pull*, you can make sure you aren't forfeiting a valuable piece of the equation.

- If your own logic is wrong, *pull* will expose where you've gone off the path. It will keep you from embarrassing yourself.

Logic and Passion Are Not Sufficient

Here's a statement you can take to the bank: *People will tolerate your conclusions and act on their own.*

You may be able, by the force of your logic or the strength of your passion, to get customers to nod their heads. But when they walk away from you, they will act on their own conclusions, not yours.

This is bad for sales.

In Sales, Trust = Speed

In contrast, understanding that is won through the pull process creates the *one feeling* that determines sales success: trust.

Without trust, no products get sold and no money moves from your customer's wallet to yours. And as W. Edward Deming famously formulated it, *"Trust = Speed."*

• When trust is in place, decisions are made quickly and executed without friction.

• When trust is absent, people sit across the table from you, recognize your product as great, and say, "We better think about this for a bit. How about we get back to you?"

We love a story from *The Speed of Trust*[*] by Stephen R. Covey (Stephen Covey's son) about a New York street vendor who sells superb coffee and fresh donuts.

---

[*] Stephen R. Covey, *The Speed of Trust: The One Thing That Changes Everything* (New York: Simon & Schuster Audio, 2006).

Because of the quality of this vendor's goods, people were lining up twenty deep at his stand. But however hard the vendor worked to serve them efficiently, some would look at their watch in exasperation and leave.

He was losing business. What to do?

The vendor analyzed his processes and pinpointed where the bottleneck was. He was already pouring coffee and dispensing donuts as quickly as he could. It was making change that was consuming too much time.

So he decided to make a risky move. He put out a basket with a sign that said, "Place your money here." Some people thought he was crazy. Trust people in downtown New York and you're just *asking* to be ripped off.

But that's not what happened.

A coffee and a donut cost $2.25. Most people threw three bucks in without taking the time to dig around for their change. What's more, many people told the vendor they loved the speedy new system and appreciated the fact that he trusted them.

Some of them threw in a five-dollar bill. They were repaying him for his expression of trust.

Some people did abuse the system, but only a small percentage. The vendor was way ahead of the game in every respect, because trust = speed.

We at Juice Inc. have customer relationships where trust is high. The decision maker talks to us about a major piece of work and we ask, "Do you need us to write up a proposal for this?" "Oh, no need to do that," is the reply. "Just send us the contract."

This decision saves us a full day of proposal writing. A day that may be applied to going after new business. A lovely example of how trust = speed.

Here's where the hard-edged, bottom-line results of pull can show up in your career. There's a major relationship between understanding and trust. As Bill Bachrach and Karen Risch put it in their book *Values-Based Selling*:[*]

> People don't trust you because they understand you ... they trust you because *you understand them.*

That makes sense. It's probably difficult for you to trust someone who misunderstands you.

In fact, there's an integral relationship between understanding and trust. The deeper the understanding, the more trust created. Why? Because feeling understood is one of our primal needs.

Consider what Swiss psychiatrist Paul Tournier says about this in his book *To Understand Each Other*[**]:

> It is impossible to overemphasize the immense need we have to be really listened to, to be taken seriously, to be understood ... No one can develop freely in this world and find a full life without feeling understood by at least one person.

When someone meets a need that is as primal as the need to feel understood, trust results.

---

[*] Bill Bachrach and Karen Risch, *Values-Based Selling: The Art of Building High-Trust Relationships* (San Diego: Aim High Publishing, 1996).
[**] Paul Tournier, *To Understand Each Other* (Louisville: Westminster/John Knox Press, 1967).

We will delve more deeply into this process in the next chapter, by unpacking the two major components of Pull Conversations.

What Are We Really Saying Here?

- You can distinguish yourself from two-thirds of salespeople by pulling first rather than pushing first.

- The most crucial preparatory step in getting people to understand you is to create capacity in them through Pull Conversations.

- Push conversations blind you to your customers' sticking points. Pull Conversations reveal them.

- People act on their own conclusions, not yours.

- Pull helps you understand your customers' conclusions and reveal to them how you can bring appropriate value.

Put the Sticking Point to Work

Slow yourself down in your next sales conversation. Pull out what's important to your customer. Play that back to them in order to build trust. Be willing to see the payoff in your next conversation with this customer.

Chapter 5

THE KEY COMPONENTS
OF PULL

Combining Inquiry and Directness

Pull is a blend of two "heart-sets" that work well together to help you detect your customer's sticking point. I'm talking about inquiry and directness.

Inquiry

Inquiry was made popular in the fifth century B.C. by a fellow named Socrates. It is the drive to deeply understand another person's reality.

Inquiry goes far beyond openness or showing interest. It takes these elements a step further, into the new terrain of raw need. "I *need* to know your viewpoint. I *need* to know what's going on in your world. I *need* to understand what drives you."

Like a magnet, inquiry powerfully attracts clarity to itself. Inquiry goes far beyond asking questions. It enables undivided focus, strips away ambiguity, and comes back with the trophy: the essence of what the customer is really trying to express.

Directness

Directness is a strong drive to be refreshingly real: to get to reality as quickly as possible. Directness enables you assert your reality to others face to face, as opposed to the indirect approach: sending your message in couched terms or through an indirect medium like e-mail.

Directness transcends most people's definition of honesty (telling the truth). It takes you to a place of *not withholding* what's going on inside you. Directness means being open to telling your truth, to putting it out there into the world.

Naturally, your discernment filter needs to be on. Naturally, you need to determine how, when, and what information to share and with whom to share it.

There's an element of passion in directness that makes an imprint on your customers. As you will see in chapter 9, it is critical for you as a salesperson to go beyond facts and learn to share your message using stories and symbols — the language of emotion.

Jim Rohn, America's business philosopher, is fond of saying:

Effective communication is 20% what you know and 80% *how you feel about what you know.*

The matrix on page 43 shows how inquiry and directness work together in conversation. When they're both fully present, you can:

- Detect the sticking point.

- Identify the emotional energizer.

- Craft a solution that works for both of you.

Directness is a strong desire to be understood. It is marked by frankness, persuasion, authenticity, honesty, candor, reality, advocacy, and passion.

Inquiry is a strong desire to be understood. It is marked by openness, intense curiosity, humility, a learner's heart, searching, vulnerability, empathy, exploration, and the desire to discover others' frames of reference.

Some salespeople have a strong drive to understand their customers. I use the word *inquiry* to capture this drive, as well.

What are the traits of people who are strong at inquiry?

- They tend to be open-minded, non-judgmental, intensely curious, and empathetic. They're good at perspective taking — at seeing the other person's frame of reference.

- They tend to be good at the discovery and exploration aspects of conversation.

"Listens hard" is a good way to describe how these people behave.

Pull Matrix

Pull
- significant understanding
- significant trust
- significant reality
(Bigger Reality)

Push
- little understanding
- little trust
- little reality

Acquiesce
- some understanding
- some trust
- some reality

Withdraw
- no understanding
- no trust
- no reality

▶ DIRECTNESS
a strong desire to be understood, marked by:
frankness, persuasion, authenticity, honesty, candor, reality, advocacy, and passion

▶ INQUIRY
a strong desire to understand, marked by: openness, intense curiosity, humility, a learner's heart, searching, vulnerability, empathy, exploration, and discovery of others' frames of reference

Perhaps you have a drive to understand. Or perhaps you have the other drive: to be understood. We use the word *directness* to capture this second drive.

Don't you just love people who are respectfully direct? They are frank and candid. They are honest, real, and authentic. They speak their truth in a straightforward manner. You always know where you stand with them.

"Talks straight" is a good way to describe how such people behave.

Both of these drives are valuable in sales.

But what happens if you exercise one at the expense of the other?

- If you're strong at inquiry but don't step up and speak your truth, your customers experience you as an aquiesce salesperson. You understand their needs and concerns, but you fail to make your own needs and concerns understood. You will most likely lose their respect, as a result.

- If you're strong at directness but fail to inquire deeply into the customer's frame of reference, your customers experience you as a *push* salesperson. Your persuasion skills may win the argument but lose the sale. Why? Because *people will tolerate your conclusions and act on their own conclusions.*

When you push without fully understanding your customer, trust is likely to take a hit. And selling is what you have to do when insufficient trust exists in the relationship. When trust is strong, all you have to do is make a recommendation and your customers will take action

If you lack inquiry and directness in your sales work, your customers will think, "This person is withdrawing. Time to shut this relationship down." You may want to consider a career in poetry or art. It will be tough for you to create value for your customers if you lack the drive to understand their needs or the drive to make your own needs understood.

Blended Is Splendid: Inquiry *and* Directness

Now here's a provocative question: What if you could blend inquiry and directness?

What if you could show up with a strong drive to understand what's most important to your customer *and* a strong drive to help them understand what's important to you?

The answer is this: Your customers will experience you as a pull salesperson. Through pull you will find out what's really going on beneath the surface with your customers, and you will educate them in the value you can create for them.

And we've discovered something else about pull that will juice any professional salesperson:

Pull draws the Bigger Reality to the surface. The Bigger Reality is the surprising solution that is greater than anything you or the customer could have engineered or anticipated.

Conversations that are one way and do not add value happen in the quadrants where inquiry and directness are not fully present.

The only time a Bigger Reality can emerge is when two people show up with both inquiry and directness, and, in the case of both people, neither is functioning at the expense of the other.

How Inquiry and Directness Work Together

Take a look at how inquiry and directness both show up in the following examples.

- When David senses his customer digging in, he asks, "Is there something about our product or our approach that makes you uncomfortable using us?"

- Before writing a proposal, Robin asks her primary contact, "Can you tell me about the key decision makers and what their criteria are for making the buying decision?"

- Damian says something offensive in a sales meeting. Melissa approaches him afterward and says, "Damian, I have concerns about your comment in the meeting, but first I'd like to understand your rationale. Then I'll share my concerns."

- When Jason loses the business, he asks his key contact, "Are you at liberty to tell me who you awarded the business to and what it was about their approach that caused you to choose them over us?"

Why is it important to blend inquiry and directness? Because customers don't always say what they mean. Neither do they always mean what they say. Asking straightforward questions with an empathetic tone is the best way to make your relationship real.

Here's another example:

- A customer, Gunther, loses his child in a tragic bike accident. When he returns to work, most of the salespeople he deals with are "business only," skirting what happened. Jill is a salesperson who has a moderately close relationship with Gunther. She books a lunch with him and says, "Gunther, I have no idea what you must be going through at this time, but I do know from experience that it can be helpful to talk. Can I ask you how you're doing?"

"Other Than That"

Paul McCallum, a friend and successful salesperson I know, uses a phrase that allows him to exhibit the blend of inquiry and directness. When a customer brings up a concern, Paul addresses it and then penetrates further by asking, "Other than that, is there anything else that is keeping you from moving forward?"

This clearly demonstrates to the customer that Paul is unflinching in his desire for realism and in his seriousness about meeting their needs.

Think of the blend as:

- Asking penetrating questions diplomatically.

- Mixing respectful honesty with intense curiosity.

- Asking hard questions in a soft way.

- Speaking your truth in a way that fits the other's world.

- Listening hard and talking straight.

Remember my story in chapter 1 about pulling the electrical cord through the hose? Pull is like a string. You can use it to pull out what's happening in your customer's world (inquiry). Or you can use it to pull your customer into your world (directness).

In the following chapters, you will see practical examples of how you can blend inquiry and directness to reach mutual understanding with your customers.

What Are We Really Saying Here?

• Great salespeople exhibit a blend of inquiry and directness that produces trust and respect.

  ◦ Inquiry wins them the customer's trust.

  ◦ Directness wins them their respect.

• Although deep and thorough listening is definitely a component of Pull Conversations, these conversations are more than that. Pull Conversations are a very direct, active type of inquiry that slices through assumptions and perceptions because it *has* to get to reality.

Put the Sticking Point to Work

Take a moment to plot your sales style on the matrix on page 43. What's your growth edge? Do you need to bring more inquiry or more directness into your sales relationships? As you call on clients this week, focus your attention on developing the element that's more in need of growth.

Chapter 6

STEP INTO YOUR CUSTOMER'S WORLD

Understanding Their Reality

We've seen that Pull Conversations have a logic to them. When you blend inquiry and directness, you discover what drives your customer's decisions.

But what if your customer's core emotional energizer is hidden? How do you pull it out to the surface?

By stepping into your customer's world to detect the energizer that is most important to them. This chapter shows you how.

One Salesperson's Transformation

Much to the envy of his peers, car salesman Rob LeBlanc is getting lots of lay downs — sales at full price — at the car dealership where he works. Getting to the place where your customers trust you enough to give you lay downs is the dream of everyone who sells cars.

Why does this happen for Rob so often? Because he has discovered the secret of successful sales. He knows that stepping into his customers' world and seeing their reality is the quickest way to get this kind of result.

"It wasn't always that way," Rob says. "I was way too uptight when I started off. I would meet the customer and immediately jump into my blurb: the hundred hot things I thought they should know about the car.

"I ended up saying things that were not valuable to them and wondered why they balked when I went for the close. In many cases I think I was actually confusing or frustrating them out of the sale."

Rob winces at the memory. "I lost some deals and elongated others. Worse yet, price turned into the biggest decision-making factor — just the thing you don't want."

Rob faced a choicepoint early in his career. The salesman who was achieving the highest volume of sales at his dealership did so through forceful push sales techniques. He used guilt to strong-arm people into buying. Rob asked himself whether he was going to pattern himself after this sales guy to get quick results.

Fortunately, he saw through his colleague as a man who got the numbers but rarely any repeat customers.

Rob had a hunch that repeat customers were the key to long-term success. He decided to use exactly the opposite approach. He would be:

- Easygoing.

- Low pressure.

- Respectful.

- Understanding of his customers' specific needs.

- Helpful to customers by showing them how he could meet those needs

Rob began to learn that simple questions unlocked the sales process. He started asking customers, "What's important to you in a car? What did you like about your last vehicle?"

Every question pulled out responses that helped him step into his customer's world. Soon he understood their specific definition of value.

- Beneath the desire for performance, Rob saw the emotional energizer of adventure.

- Beneath the desire for aesthetics, he saw the energizer of meaning.

- Beneath safety and theft protection, he saw security.

- Beneath maintenance, he saw freedom.

This allowed Rob to do three things:

1. Point the customer to exactly the right vehicle.

2. Highlight the benefits of the vehicle that mattered most to the customer.

3. Do so in language that had a quick and lasting impact.

Next, Rob invested time in a leisurely test drive, which allowed him to say:

- "Now, you said that performance was important for you. Why don't you put your foot down on the gas pedal and see what this thing will do off the line?"

- "You were asking about protection for your kids. If your little girl was back here where I'm sitting and the vehicle was hit from the side, here's exactly how the side air bags would provide maximum security for her."

By the time the test drive was over, his customer felt Rob deeply understood their reality.

The net result for Rob? By spending this kind of time up front, he spent little time in the price negotiation phase.

And what did he do when a sticking point showed up in this phase? He resorted to the techniques of Pull Conversations. He pulled the string attached to the sticking point of price, which led him to the customer's core emotional need, or energizer.

Rob knew that pulling on that string would lead him to what was most important to his customer. Then he could frame his offer in a way that appealed to their interests.

Relationship Tension and Task Tension

Think about Rob's story in terms of relationship tension and task tension.

Jodi is in the market for a car. Is her level of relationship tension high or low when she first meets Rob? Typically it is high.

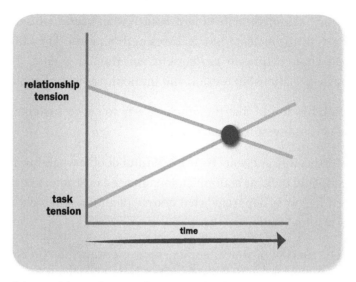

(This model compliments of Paul McCallum)

"Is this guy going to try to push something on me that I don't need?"

Is her task tension (her need to decide and take action) high or low? Typically, it is very low. She has no desire to act until she is absolutely sure she can trust Rob.

Everything Rob does with Jodi is designed to completely reverse this situation: *to create a customer environment where relationship tension is reduced and task tension is increased.*

Make these two lines intersect and you arrive at a beautiful dot where you get the sale.

To what extent do you follow this simple but powerful approach with your customers?

How much time does it take you to get to the dot?

Many salespeople, feeling pressure to get results quickly, jump right to *pushing* out features and benefits. They don't invest enough time in *pulling* out emotions and data. This increases relationship tension and immobilizes task tension.

Rob has found that the quickest way to get to sustainable results is to invest the time to pull.

Do this well and you create a beautiful double whammy: less tension and quicker action. Understand the customer's reality and it becomes apparent what course of action will yield the best results.

The concept of understanding, then, is critical. You probably use the word many times a day. Do you know what it actually means? The next story unpacks a great working definition for this powerful but often misunderstood word.

A Tale of the Roses

Sometimes it helps to think about sales relationships by thinking about non-sales ones.

Imagine that you have a neighbor, Maria, who is a rose fanatic. Her life revolves around roses. She talks about roses, thinks about roses, and spends all her time, money, and energy on roses.

Now, you're not against flowers. Like many people, you have a few flowerbeds yourself. But inwardly you believe Maria is a little over the top with her rose obsession.

One day you're having a conversation with Maria over the hedge. She's gushing about how beautiful her roses are. Not wanting to get drawn into a lengthy account of the latest flower show, you shut the conversation down and walk away, wondering, "What *is* it about these roses that captivates her so?"

Awhile later you are looking out your kitchen window. You can see the back of a few roses as you peer through Maria's hedge.

Because you're interested in getting better at pulling out other people's realities, you decide it's time to find out why Maria loves roses so much. You step out of your house and make the trek to Maria's door. As you knock on her door, you wonder what you may be getting yourself into.

Once you're seated and into your conversation, you say, "Maria, I know you are passionate about roses but I've never taken the time to find out why. I'd really like to know why you love them so much."

Maria leads you to her kitchen and throws open the window. The sight and the smell of the roses hit you with equal force.

Next, she begins to tell you about her earliest memories, of helping her mother in her rose garden back in Yugoslavia. The fondest memories of her life come from those moments with her mother in that lush garden.

Then Maria tells you something deeper behind her memories. Her mother was killed in the ethnic battles of her country. The rose garden not only reminds her of good times with her mother, it also serves as a memorial to her mother's memory. Maria's garden helps her deal with her grief.

Now that you see and feel Maria's reality and her rose obsession makes sense to you, you face a choicepoint: Do you reflect your newfound understanding back to Maria, or do you simply let her finish telling her story and walk out of her house?

The more appropriate behavior is to reflect back to Maria what you have understood her to say.

"Now I know why you love roses so much," you might say, "I am deeply touched by your love for your mother and how you are honoring her. Thank you for sharing this experience with me."

Maria is honored that you spent the time to hear her story. And your views about the amount of time and energy she spends with her roses have undergone a massive shift.

What did it take for you to gain this understanding? You had to take several actions:

- Exit your house.

- Walk down your driveway.

- Walk on the sidewalk toward Maria's house.

- Walk up her driveway.

- Climb her steps.

- Knock on her door.

- Ask if you could come in.

- Walk into her house.

- Listen to her.

But if you had to reduce all those actions into two main actions, what would they be?

- The first action was *stepping out of your world.*

- The second was *stepping into her world.* When you did so, it became relatively easy to see her reality the way she sees it and to reflect back to her what you now saw more clearly.

This story offers us a working definition for the word *understanding.* To understand is *to step into another's world, see their reality, and reflect back what you have seen.*

We have helped thousands of people acquire this skill. The process has convinced us that you cannot step into someone else's world until you first leave your own.

Why don't we do this? Why is this so hard? What are *our* sticking points?

Our world is a place of security. It is comfortable. It is safe. The thought of stepping outside frightens us.

To be successful as salespeople, we have to make our customer's world our primary focus. And we have to make our need to get the sale our secondary focus.

This is not common practice. I have asked participants all over North America, "How many of you had parents or teachers who taught you how to step into someone else's world and see their reality?" Fewer than 10% say they have.

Perhaps you feel the same way. The good news is that it's not too late to learn this crucial life skill. The better news is that doing so can make a difference in some of the thorniest customer situations you may have to face.

What Are We Really Saying Here?

- The skill of understanding another's reality is more instrumental than any other in sales success.

- Caring about your customer's needs builds trust — and repeat business.

- When a customer feels deeply heard, they will be more open to your own goals.

- To step into someone's world, you have to be able to step out of your own.

- To do that, you have to shift from self-centeredness to other-centeredness.

Put the Sticking Point to Work

The car salesman Rob LeBlanc sees a desire for adventure beneath concerns about performance. He sees a desire for significance beneath concerns about aesthetics. Jot down your customers' typical concerns and the core emotional energizers that drive them.

Chapter 7

THE MAGIC OF UNDERSTANDING
Transforming Conflicts into
Sales Opportunities

We have been exploring how Pull Conversations can transform your sales relationships. This chapter shows how these conversations can transform *conflicts* between salespeople and customers into sales opportunities.

Finding Common Ground

Ben is a pet food sales rep who calls on stores like Wal-Mart and other large retailers. Once, when checking out his product displays at a Wal-Mart store, he discovered that his competitor's product was being prominently showcased on an end-cap.

This wouldn't have concerned Ben except for one vital fact: This particular end-cap was supposed to be his. It was a premier piece of shelf space that his head office had recently negotiated with Wal-Mart.

Ben went searching for the store manager.

"Hi, Antonio. I see Puppy-Love's product is being displayed on this end-cap. My plan-o-gram shows that my product is supposed to be there. Do you think we could get it changed over?"

"That's not likely to happen soon. We have a lot going on right now and I'm short on people."

"But our head office has an agreement with your head office for this space. You're obligated by contract to put my product up there. If you need me to go back into inventory, get my product, and re-face these shelves, I'd be willing to do it."

"Our policy won't permit you to go into inventory. Only our employees can go back there."

"But I go into all the other Wal-Marts' inventories. Nobody else has a problem with it."

"Maybe so, but you're not going into mine."

"So how do I make sure my product gets on this end-cap?"

"We'll get to it when we get to it."

"Well, that's not good enough for me. I'm going to have to get my head office to call your head office and deal with this issue."

"Do whatever you want. You're never touching the inventory in my store."

Exit Ben, smoke coming out of his ears.

You can predict how this is going to end. Even if his head office is successful in getting Wal-Mart to take action against one of their managers, Ben has accomplished nothing but win himself an enemy who's going to stonewall him at every turn.

Ben forgot one crucial truth: *People's negative emotions intensify to the extent that you fail to acknowledge them.*

Antonio's negative feelings about lack of staffing and salespeople trespassing in his warehouse inventory were early sticking points that could have led Ben to his core emotional energizer: power.

Thankfully, Ben is a relatively self-aware sales rep.

That evening he felt bad about the outcome of his conversation with Antonio. He thought about what he could have done differently.

He told me, during one of my training sessions, the conclusion he came to.

"I didn't pull. I blew right by his two sticking points: that he was short on staff and that he wanted control. I pushed, and the wire definitely got stuck in the hose. I knew I needed to go back there the next day and do things differently."

Here's how the sales conversation went.

"Antonio, I owe you an apology," Ben said. "I know you must be busy, but can we talk for a moment?"

"I guess so."

"Thank you. I was out of line yesterday and I blew it. I'm sorry for my behavior."

"Okay ..."

"If I was in your shoes, I would have been thinking, 'Who does this guy think he is, telling me he's going to go back into my inventory?' I'm not surprised our conversation didn't go well."

"I won't lie to you — you did get under my skin."

"If I understand your reality as a manager, you've got some pretty big staffing limitations that make it tough for you to get everything out when you'd like to. Have I got that right?"

"You better believe it."

"And you take the security of your inventory very seriously and are a guy who plays by the rules."

"Absolutely."

"And I didn't acknowledge either of those challenges yesterday in my approach with you."

"That's true."

"Well, I thought hard about those two things last night. I want to tell you that I have some real appreciation for your challenges."

"That's good."

"I also think you and I have some common ground here."

"What would that be?"

"We both want your store to be successful and we both want a headache-free relationship. Would you agree?"

"Absolutely."

"Is there any way we can both get what we want here? We both know my product sells well when it's displayed prominently. What if I could work with one of your newer employees to get the product out? Of course I wouldn't go near inventory, but I've got a lot of experience in product display and you would benefit by having me coach your employee in that. I would get the benefit of knowing my product is being well displayed."

"I think I could go for something like that."

"Can we set something up for later this week?"

"Sure. Why don't you give me a call and I'll have an employee ready to help you."

Real Customer Appreciation

It's amazing, but *customers will make concessions for you, accommodate you, even make sacrifices for you as long as they feel you understand and appreciate their sacrifices.*

However, the instant they sense that you don't understand and appreciate what they do for you, their goodwill will dry up. Any prospect of customer engagement will evaporate in a heartbeat.

The key to understanding and appreciation is to be able to identify the underlying messages in any conversation.

What Are We Really Saying Here?

- Acknowledging a customer's negative feelings reduces their resistance to you.

- Framing a sale in terms of both parties' goals helps tame conflict.

Put the Sticking Point to Work

In the story above, Antonio's core emotional energizer was power. What is the core emotional energizer of your most challenging customer? Call on this customer and practice acknowledging and reflecting back the emotions you've left unacknowledged in the past. (See more on reflection in the next chapter.)

Chapter 8

REFLECT THE CUSTOMER'S REALITY
Optimizing Your Sales Effectiveness

Pull Conversations will require you and enable you to stretch beyond the rudiments of active listening. By stepping into the other person's world and feeling what they feel, you'll be able to close the loop, using what I call the *implication reflection*.

The implication reflection involves reflecting back not only the person's feeling but also the implications of what that feeling means to them in their specific situation.

Reflection

Reflection is one of the best ways to honor your customers. It demonstrates to them that you value what they *say* and understand what they *mean*.

When light hits a mirror, the light ray is absorbed by a layer of glass and then reflected back by the polished silver on the back of the glass. When we listen well, we do the same thing. We absorb the person's thoughts, process them, and then reflect them back accurately.

If you do this well, your customer should be able to instantly recognize their essence in your reflection.

This is a great form of honor, as a story, in Kerry L. Johnson's book *Sales Magic*, illustrates.*

It seems that a friend of Johnson's was fortunate to have I.M. Pei, the famous architect, as a seatmate on a cross-country flight. This friend was a native of Boston and had always admired Pei's John Hancock Building in Copley Square, a building that sits between two nineteenth-century marvels, Trinity Church and the Boston Public Library.

Johnson's friend asked the architect why he sheathed the Hancock building in glass when it sat between two buildings made of stone and granite.

"Well, when you look into that glass, what do you see?" Pei replied.

"Why, I — I see the two magnificent buildings!"

"Exactly."

Pull Conversations create a connection with the customer's reality by reflecting it back accurately. The art of reflecting

---

* Kerry L. Johnson, *Sales Magic: Revolutionary New Techniques That Will Double Your Results* (New York: HarperCollins, 1995).

makes you someone people trust to *re-present* themselves to themselves. Reflecting is at the heart of what is called active or empathic listening.

How to Listen Empathically

Empathy is the ability to feel what someone is feeling without their having to tell you. Empathy, in fact, means "passion in." Listening empathically is the process of getting someone else's feelings *in you*, then closing the loop by reflecting them back.

There are two levels of empathy.

- *Intellectual empathy* is basically perspective taking: the ability to accurately perceive another's point of view.

- *Emotional empathy* is becoming imprinted with and vicariously experiencing the emotions of another person.

Both types of empathy are valuable. However, if empathy is not your strong suit, you will be best served by cultivating intellectual empathy first. Going on from there to develop your emotional empathy will produce a big payoff: People will feel deeply understood by you and connected to you.

It shouldn't have to be said, but we have learned that it's necessary to do so: This skill should be used only in the service of others, never to manipulate or exploit them.

To listen empathically, use your ears to capture the info stream and your eyes and "gut" to detect the emotions from the meaning stream.

People's nonverbals are the most reliable tip-off to their feelings. The body tends to tell the truth. For example watch:

- Their eyes.

- Their hands.

- Their posture.

These will typically broadcast the truth. It's easy for a person to distort with their words; it's difficult for them to do so with their body.

The Three Components of Empathic Listening

To listen empathically, you need three basic components, preferably framed in your own words.

1. *A tentative statement*: It sounds like ...

2. *The essence of the feeling*: ... you're angry ...

3. *The implications inside their world*: ... because our sales presentation disturbed your boss.

Here are two short examples:

Tentative statement: Let me play this back to you ...

The essence: ... you're concerned about our ability to hit the November deadline ...

The implications: ... and what this might mean for the credibility of your team.

Tentative statement: So what I've heard you say is ...

The essence: ... that you're disappointed with what our design team has come up with ...

The implications: ... and it has impacted your confidence about the long-term success of the project.

From Beginner to Master Reflector

There are three levels of sophistication when it comes to reflection:

- A *sales beginner* can reflect back the exact words of the customer. The customer may actually find this irritating, but simple *restating* is better to them than no reflection at all.

- A *sales intermediate* can hear the customer say many things and reflect back the essence of the message in their own words.

- A *master salesperson* can hear all the customer says and reflect back not only the essence of the customer's message, but also what it means to them: what the implications are inside their world.

Don't Walk in Their Shoes

You've no doubt heard someone say, "Put yourself in the other person's shoes." I applaud the intent of this adage, but it often causes salespeople to make some serious blunders.

In his book *Let's Get Real or Let's Not Play,** Mahan Khalsa tells a great story about his business partner Ron in a meeting with a customer.

The customer asked, "How big are you guys?"

Putting *himself* in his customer's shoes and feeling the concern about scalability, Ron began to push *size*. He painted an inflated picture of the size and scope of his (rather small) business.

When Ron had finished, the customer responded with:

That's too bad. We're a small fish that's been swimming in a big pond of a very big supplier. Our account means almost nothing to them and that shows up in the service they've been giving us. We just made a strategic decision to be a big fish in a small supplier's pond — one we would mean a lot to — one that will be more attuned to our needs. Sorry, but it looks like you guys are too big for us.

Oops. Ron put himself inside his customer's shoes, *but it was still Ron inside the customer's shoes*: Ron with all his assumptions, beliefs, and conclusions.

A salesperson's baggage determines how they see their customer's world. If you put yourself with all your baggage inside the customer's shoes, you have a very slim chance of accurately understanding their core emotional needs.

---

* Mahan Khalsa and Randy Illig, *Let's Get Real or Let's Not Play: Transforming the Buyer/Seller Relationship*, revised and updated (New York: Portfolio/Penguin Group, 2008).

This is why we use the language "step into the customer's world so you can see and feel their reality."

The question is, what can you do to optimize your effectiveness in this way?

1. Develop an awareness of your own beliefs and how you might be projecting them onto your customer:

   ◆ "Customers want lower prices."

   ◆ "Customers want big, established vendors."

   ◆ "Customers don't want me to talk to them about my personal life."

2. Use the power of your mind's eye to imagine what it might feel like for your customer in the midst of their situation. Check with them to see if you've visualized correctly. This, in essence, is the implication reflection.

3. Ask more questions before you formulate your answer.

   Here's where pull can really serve you:

   ◆ You hear the question, "How big are you guys?"

   ◆ You *pull* by asking, "I'd love to tell you about the size of our organization, but just to ensure that I don't waste your time with redundant information, can you tell me what it is about size that's most important to you in your current situation?"

How many times could a little bit of pull have saved a sale for you?

Think about a recent sales call. When the customer asked you a question about *x*, did you have an instant comeback ready for them, instead of asking, "Can you tell me what it is about *x* that is most important to you?" If your answer is yes, you need to shift from push to pull.

What Are We Really Saying Here?

- Go beyond active listening and reflect back not only the customer's feeling but also the implications of that feeling.

- Don't put *yourself* in the customer's shoes. Step into their world and see and feel their reality the way *they* see it.

Put the Sticking Point to Work

Tomorrow, focus your attention on the number of times that you're able to "reflect the implication" in interactions with your customers, your spouse, or your children.

Chapter 9

THE POWER OF INVITATIONAL LANGUAGE

Welcoming Customers into Your World

The three chapters previous to this focused on the skill of stepping into your customer's world to pull out what's most important to them. This chapter explores how you can invite your customer into your world so they can gain a clear picture of how you create value for them.

See, Feel, Change

When two people *see* and *feel* each other's realities, big things can happen. Harvard change expert John Kotter describes this phenomenon in his book *The Heart of Change*.[*] He recalls how he used to believe that what people needed was analysis. Analysis

---

[*] John P. Kotter and Dan S. Cohen, *The Heart of Change: Real-Life Stories of How People Change Their Organization* (Boston: Harvard Business School Press, 2002.)

would make them think differently, and thinking differently would make them change.

After years of experience, he learned that the reliable sequence was not analyze, think, change. It was see, feel, change.

* People see something compelling and experience a powerful feeling in their gut.

* That feeling moves them to a place of embracing change: moving toward the solution that you're offering them.

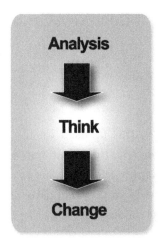 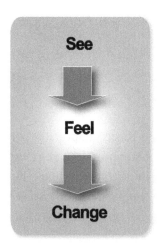

Source – The Heart of Change, John Kotter

Kotter tells a great story of a large manufacturing organization in which purchasing had clearly gotten out of hand. Individual plants all insisted on doing their own purchasing. The waste in the system was hemorrhaging company profits to the tune of $200 million a year.

As a head-office leader, Jon Stegner had an idea but needed the right approach to sell it to the division presidents.

Stegner had a summer student go to all of the plants and bring back every type of glove that the plants had purchased, marking the price paid for each pair. After the student had collected the gloves from the plants, he had her pile all 424 pairs on the boardroom table.

Then he invited the division presidents into the boardroom. As Kotter tells it:

> They looked at two [pairs of gloves] that seemed exactly alike, yet one was marked $3.22 and the other $10.55. It's a rare event when these people don't have anything to say. But this day, they just stood with their mouths gaping.

The glove demonstration was put on a traveling road show to every division and dozens of plants. It reinforced throughout the organization just how bad the problem of duplication was.

The exercise sparked a mandate for change that saved the organization a great deal of money.

What about you? How can you use this powerful see, feel, change dynamic to invite customers into your world?

The first thing to note is: *People are not changed by information. They are changed by interactions with other people.*

Customers typically aren't swayed from resistance to non-resistance by information. They're swayed by the interactions they have with a person they trust.

Remember, when it comes to changing a customer's mindset, trust = speed.

Here's where we begin to see some of the transformational power of Pull Conversations. When done well, these conversations enable customers to embrace change more quickly than perhaps anything else can. So let's focus on what you can do to invite others into your reality, where they can *see and feel* the opportunities involved in working with you.

Invite Them into Your World

There are two ways to invite someone into your world.

- The first is to simply ask them to listen to you. Then, when you know you've stepped into someone's world, seen their reality, and reflected it back to their satisfaction and they still aren't showing any signs of trying to understand you, it's time to be direct and make your needs known in a straightforward way: "I think I understand your point of view now. May I share mine?"

- The second is to use invitational language that makes your perspective come alive for them: language that intrigues them and is easy for them to relate to.

Use Language That Lives

Stories, metaphors, analogies, and illustrations are effective means of inviting a person into your world. These communication tools not only create a curiosity in the mind and heart of your listener, they also make a lasting imprint.

You know this. Think of the data bytes that have riveted themselves to your memory. They probably came to you framed in "story."

It's good to be reminded of this story dynamic. It helps us avoid the danger of slipping into a one-dimensional communication style. One that's all facts and no emotions or symbols.

Consider what Boyd Clarke and Ron Crossland say on this point in their book *The Leader's Voice*:

> When your intent is to move people to action, to help them understand and deepen their appreciation and gain more insight and more passion about their work, you have got to have all three [media]: facts, emotion, and symbols.

Clarke and Crossland call symbols "shorthand ways of conveying both emotion and meaning." He adds that although facts are vital, they lack meaning and impact until we blend them with emotions and symbols. As he puts it:

> Adding the other two channels in the appropriate ways at the appropriate times dramatically increases the chance of the communication getting through.

Use Stories as a Springboard
Stephen Denning, author of *The Springboard*, worked in the World Bank. He was charged with implementing a knowledge-management solution that would serve the organization's employees around the globe.

---

* Boyd Clarke and Ron Crossland, *The Leader's Voice: How Your Communication Can Inspire Action and Get Results!* (New York: The Tom Peters Press and SelectBooks, 2002).
** Stephen Denning, *The Springboard: How Storytelling Ignites Action in Knowledge-Era Organizations* (Butterworth-Heinemann, 2002).

In theory, this online repository of acquired wisdom had great appeal. In practice, it was a monumental task, made next to impossible by the stalwart stubbornness of change-resistant decision makers throughout the bank.

Denning amassed a persuasive set of statistics and studies and embedded them in an impressive PowerPoint presentation. He met with constituents of the bank globally, walking group after group through his impassioned appeal for an ironclad knowledge-management system.

He made it very clear that the system he was proposing would give World Bank employees the information they needed in a matter of moments, no matter what continent they were on. The response was always the same: "It looks like an interesting idea, but we don't think it will work here."

Then Denning heard a story that grabbed his attention. It was an account of a Zambian health-care worker who was trying to treat a case of malaria. Out in the middle of nowhere, he logged onto the website of the Centers for Disease Control in Atlanta, Georgia. In moments, he was able to procure the exact information needed to successfully treat the patient.

Denning wondered what would happen if he simply told people the story of the Zambian health-care worker. How would they respond?

He told the story at his next meeting. The response stunned him.

"Hey, imagine if we could do something like that," one participant said. "Our employees could log on and get the information they needed to serve our customers.

It wouldn't matter where they were or what time zone they were in. Why couldn't we implement something like this?"

This simple story made more of an impact in two minutes than all his statistics, studies, and PowerPoint presentations had in two hours.

When people saw themselves inside this story, they were able to *see and feel* the implications of making data accessible to everyone in the organization everywhere.

Denning went on to tell the story across the World Bank. It won the day, transforming staunch resistors into impassioned champions of the process he was recommending.

Feelings produced the change.

Use Stories to Frame Solutions
What stories do you use? Your sales approach needs to be built on compelling narratives that intrigue your customer.

- We often tell the story of "Bill," the engineer with stunted emotional intelligence who, after our coaching, saved his organization a verified $1.2 million through his use of Pull Conversations.

- We talk about the CEO who heard people singing out on the manufacturing floor after his managers experienced our training.

- We share the story of the distribution center that cut its credits and returns in half within six months of working with us.

- We talk about going out with the chicken-catchers of a fast-food giant in the middle of the night because we needed a deeper understanding of the organization's awareness of animal rights in their production chain.

These stories transport the customer from his world right into ours. They render a vocabulary to our values and the results we produce. It's common for customers to respond by asking, "How? How do you do that? How would you do that here?"

In such moments we have an entrée to frame our solution. We not only have understood what's most important inside the customer's world, we also have *intrigued them into ours.*

What Are We Really Saying Here?

- Your customers feel before they think.

- People are changed by relationships, not by information.

- Stories can help you frame a sales conversation.

- Stories, images, and symbols are the best ways to help a customer see and feel your reality. And this enables them to change.

Put the Sticking Point to Work

Identify the top three stories you can use to evoke powerful feelings and intrigue your customers into your world.

Chapter 10

THE POWER OF FACE-TO-FACE CONVERSATIONS

Speaking Your Truth Productively

After you have invited the other person into your world, it's time to help them see your reality. There are two ways to do this: the first is to be direct; the second is to speak your truth productively.

Be Direct

Directness has a quality of immediacy to it that calls for conversing face-to-face whenever possible rather than resorting to less-direct forms of communication like phone or e-mail.

Face-to-face conversation is the conduit that conveys the greatest amount of emotion, trust, and understanding between people.

I'm thankful for e-mail and voice mail. I have experienced how they can make us more efficient and effective as salespeople. But I also recognize their limitations when it comes to handling the robust flow of inner resources that need to be shared between salespeople and their customers.

A big part of being effective as a communicator is knowing the best medium for specific messages.

Why Face-to-Face Conversations Release Energy

In the introduction to this book, I shared the story of an electrifying conversation with David Knechtel, showing how energy can jump from one person to another very quickly if the right conditions are present. More often than not, these conditions are created by face-to-face conversations. There are four reasons why:

• Mirror neurons.

• The emotional contagion caused by the "open loop" in our brain circuitry.

• Trust-building hormones that are released in this type of conversation.

• Our ability to quickly "click" with each other when our eyes pick up on the speaker's *nonverbal cues*.

If you want to release intelligent energy in your sales career, it's important for you to know the basics of how these four dynamics work.

Mirror Neurons

Neuroscientists can insert into your brain an electrode so laser-thin it can monitor the firing of a single neuron. This technology enables them to identify which parts of your brain fire when you execute a certain task. Clench your fist and a certain neuron lights up. Grimace and another one does.

In his book *Social Intelligence*,* Daniel Goleman reveals some intriguing discoveries about mirror neurons that can have a significant impact on our success as sales professionals:

He tells of a study in which an electrode monitored a single neuron in an awake person. Remarkably, the neuron fired both when the person anticipated pain — a pinprick — and when the person merely saw someone else receive a pinprick, providing a neural snapshot of primal empathy in action.

Our mirror neurons create a brain-to-brain linkup with others in which we mirror back the emotions or actions we sense.

Goleman shares the insights of another study:

When volunteers lie in an fMRI watching a video showing someone smile or scowl, most brain areas that activated in observers were the same as those active in the person displaying the emotion, though not as extreme.

Mirror neurons make emotions contagious, letting the feelings we witness flow through us, helping us get in synch and follow what's going on. We "feel" the other in the broadest sense of the word: sensing their sentiments,

---

* Daniel Goleman, *Social Intelligence: The New Science of Human Relationships* (New York: Bantam Books, 2006).

their movements, their sensations, their emotions as they act inside us.

Ever wonder how children can learn to walk, talk, and relate within two years of being born? It involves far more than aping the behaviors of their parents. As they watch us and listen to us, the software of their brain is created through the conduit of their mirror neurons.

Think of the implications for you. Face-to-face interactions with your customers enable you to connect with them and read them in a way you never could do by phone or e-mail. Knowing this secret, you'd be mad to have an important conversation with a customer any other way than face to face.

Emotional Contagion
You never have to be concerned about someone else's blood getting mixed with yours just because you're sitting next to them. That's because their circulatory system and yours are closed-loop systems.

The limbic system of your brain (the emotional center), in contrast, is an open-loop system. This means emotions can be contagious. As we saw above, someone's tears or their smile can trigger an involuntary sympathetic reaction in you.

In their book *Primal Leadership*,* Goleman, Boyatzis, and McKee discuss this open-loop phenomenon and describe how emotions spread between people.

They cite studies in which scientists measure the heart rate

---

* Daniel Goleman, Richard Boyatzis, and Annie McKee, *Primal Leadership: Learning to Lead with Social Intelligence* (Boston: Harvard Business School Press, 2002).

of two people as they have a good conversation. At the beginning of the conversation, their bodies are functioning at different rhythms, but fifteen minutes later "their physiological profiles look remarkably similar — a phenomenon called *mirroring*."

> Scientists describe [the limbic loop] as "interpersonal limbic regulation," whereby one person transmits signals that can alter hormone levels, cardiovascular function, sleep rhythms, and even immune function inside the body of another ... The open-loop design of the limbic system means that other people can change our very physiology — and so our emotions.

Put salespeople and customers together in face-to-face conversations and they regulate each other's emotions.

You've probably experienced this yourself. One team member's positive, buoyant mood affects one person after another until the whole team is feeling upbeat. Or one member's angry, critical mood infects the entire team.

These authors go on to say:

> This circuitry also attunes our own biology to the dominant range of feelings of the person we are with, so that our emotional states tend to converge. One term scientists use for this neural attunement is *limbic resonance*, "a symphony of mutual exchange and internal adaptation" whereby two people harmonize their emotional state.

In short, when you need to convey optimism, passion, or seriousness, your best bet is to do it face to face. As a salesperson, you send out a wavelength that your customers start resonating to. You can use this open-loop phenomenon to powerfully serve them.

Trust-Building Hormones

When trust needs to be built, use face-to-face conversation rather than defaulting to the other media. Why?

* First, face-to-face conversation increases trust, bonding, attention, and pleasure.

* Second, it reduces fear and worry.

Edward M. Hallowell puts it this way in his essay "The Human Moment at Work"*:

> Nature ... equips us with hormones that promote trust and bonding: oxytocin and vasopressin. Most abundant in nursing mothers, these hormones are always present to some degree in all of us, but they rise when we feel empathy for another person — in particular when we are meeting with someone face to face. It has been shown that these bonding hormones are at suppressed levels when people are physically separate.

This explains why it's easier to rip someone apart in an e-mail than if you were face to face with them.

Face-to-face conversations not only produce trust; they can also be the happy Prozac moments of your day. Hallowell writes:

---

* Edward M. Hallowell, "The Human Moment at Work," *Harvard Business Review*, January 1999.

Scientists hypothesize that in-person contact stimulates two important neurotransmitters: dopamine, which enhances attention and pleasure, and serotonin, which reduces fear and worry.

Just today we had a face-to-face call with a customer. At the beginning of our call, she seemed somewhat subdued. By the end of the call, she looked at us and said, "This conversation has left me totally energized."

Small wonder: She was probably experiencing a rush of conversation-induced dopamine!

Nonverbal Cues Are Meaning-Makers

Researchers long ago discovered that when people sense ambiguity between someone's verbal content and their nonverbal content, they will give more weight to the nonverbal content for the clarification they seek.

Face-to-face conversation gives you the luxury of blending your nonverbal with your verbal content. This gives your listeners the richest and most reliable mixture of meaning-making you can offer them. It allows them to "click" with you more quickly in conversation.

When your nonverbals cannot be experienced by them, they turn to their assumptions to supply the context they're missing. And, as we'll see in more detail in chapter 12, their assumptions can be the most dangerous interpreters when it comes to translating your meaning.

Don't put yourself at the mercy of people's assumptions. Choose direct, face-to-face conversations, as often as time and geography will allow. This is the quickest way to produce understanding and better results.

Being Direct Earns Respect
Being direct doesn't always create a warm, fuzzy feeling inside people, but it does create respect, clarity, and sustained results.

After conducting a session at a large conference, we were approached by an HR person from one of North America's most prestigious financial institutions. "Jerome" expressed intense interest in Juice. He felt there was a great fit between the needs of his organization and what we had to offer. He left his card with one of our salespeople and said, "Give me a call."

Two of us called Jerome a few days later and had another short but great conversation in which it was even more evident that we could add value to his organization. It was agreed that our salesperson would follow up for a lengthier investigation of his organization's needs.

Our salesman called. He called and left voice messages. He left e-mail messages. He left more voice messages. For weeks he followed up with no response.

Then he made another call. He made a very direct call to Jerome. He left this voice-mail message:

Hi, Jerome. I have no desire whatsoever to waste a minute of your time. I left our conversation on the phone a few weeks ago with a clear understanding that you wanted me to pursue a meeting with you and your group.

To be frank, I must admit that I have become frustrated with your lack of response to my e-mails and voice mails.

I would love to understand if your world has just become too crazy to do this or if something has changed for you that makes this meeting unnecessary.

I am completely fine with either a yes or a no, I just don't want to waste either of our time. Let's take five minutes on the phone to determine whether this relationship should move forward or not. You can reach me at (123) 456-7890.

The upshot of this approach was dramatic. Jerome immediately approached his VP of HR and before we knew it we were presenting to the entire group. As a result, we were offered an opportunity to deliver a session to the senior executive team and subsequently to other groups inside the organization.

People typically respect you when you're direct in a respectful way.

Ask the Unaskable

I'll never forget a conversation I had with a successful area business manager of a pharmaceutical organization. He attributed the success of his group to one simple, powerful skill: the ability to ask one tough question. He had learned that the account reps who learned to ask this question consistently outperformed their colleagues. And what was that question?

When calling on a physician who wasn't prescribing their drug, the rep was to ask, "Dr. Davis, is there something about our drug that makes you uncomfortable prescribing it?"

Nine times out of ten, this would prompt a very authentic conversation that uncovered the doctor's sticking point. When brought to the surface, many times the sticking point could be satisfactorily addressed and solved.

Some reps, however, couldn't bring themselves to ask the question. "That's too direct," they said. "It will turn the physician off." Or, "I'll be escorted out of their office."

My friend had learned something about physicians: Most of them had very little time for an indirect, roundabout approach. They appreciated respectful directness.

Are there direct questions that you believe are forbidden but which could actually unlock your success?

Why We're Not Direct
There are many reasons why people are not direct. Here are the four main ones:

- The fear of being rejected.
- The fear of hurting another's feelings.
- The fear of damaging the relationship.
- The fear of retaliation.

Each of these fears is energized by a lie that we have accepted as truth.

I know a person who doesn't speak his truth because of his fear of being hurt. Every time he had an important conversation with his dad when he was growing up, his viewpoint was disapproved, judged, and put down. He came to the conclusion, "If I speak up, I'll be rejected."

Personally, when I don't speak my truth it's because I fear I'll hurt the other person. It causes angst in me to make someone feel uncomfortable or embarrassed. I grew up believing the lie that "conflict is bad — it hurts people."

Speak Your Truth Productively

Life assumptions like these drive our behaviors in unproductive ways.

It's beyond the scope of this book to show you how to recalibrate your assumptions. Suffice it to say that your job is to get to the reality that reveals, "I do not have to give in to these fears." I'm not saying that these things will never happen to you. I'm saying that you do not have to *fear* them.

What Is Your "truth"?
Your truth is a lowercase "t" truth. We don't know any human being who has the uppercase "T" Truth. In essence, your truth is your perception of reality. It's how you see the world, yourself, and others. But even though your truth is simply your perception, it is vitally important that you speak it. As you do, you contribute to a Bigger Reality.

As the partnership with your customer evolves, you will come to many junctures where it will be critical for you to speak your truth in order to sustain customer engagement. How do you do that in a way that doesn't turn the customer off?

Use Non-Blaming Language
Let's remember the purpose of what you're doing here. You're inviting your customer into your world so they can see and feel

your reality. You don't want to do anything to shut them down or trigger a defensive response that will send them scurrying back into their own world, taking a battle stance against you.

You'll never get to the Bigger Reality if that happens.

To avoid this reaction, learn to use language that is non-blaming and non-accusatory. The essence of this approach is to speak your truth in terms of your feelings and the impact of situations on you rather than assigning a value judgment to the other's behavior.

Taking responsibility for your own feelings instead of blaming someone for making you feel a certain way does three things. It sidesteps the defensiveness of the listener, draws them inside your world, and helps them see and feel your reality.

For example, it is typically more productive to say:

- "I need to feel heard by you" than "You're not listening to me."

- "I felt disappointed" than "You let me down."

This is not to say that it's inappropriate to speak about others' behaviors. It is to say that it's critical for you to do so productively. This is done by using the xyz approach developed by marriage experts Les and Leslie Parrott. "When you do *x*, the impact is *y*. Is it possible for you to do *z* instead?"

x = Pinpoint the person's specific, observable *behavior.*

y = Identify the *impact* of that behavior.

z = Offer an acceptable *alternative* behavior.

Do not:

- Blame the person for causing your feeling.

- Judge the behavior as wrong.

- Assign a motive to the behavior.

- Demand that the other person change their behavior.

Examples of Non-Blaming XYZ Language

- "When we agree to meet and I don't find out that the meeting has been canceled till after arriving here, I find it difficult to manage my time productively. Can I ask you to give me more notice if you need to cancel our meeting?"

- "When both of our head offices create a signed agreement to display our product on the end-caps and I repeatedly find my competitor's product here instead of mine, it feels like our contract is being broken. I need to ask you to display our product where we've agreed to display it."

- "When you arrive late for a meeting with our client, we end up lacking credibility and it puts us off balance. Can I ask you to make sure you arrive on time in the future?"

- "When decisions to alter the use of our product are made without my input, it limits my ability to advocate for you in a warranty situation. Next time, can you and I consult before the decision is finalized?"

- "When you keep presenting to the client fifteen minutes past the time they agreed to give us, I believe our professionalism takes a hit. Can you keep your eye on the time and make sure you end meetings when you say you're going to?"

Naturally it's important to be aware of your tone when you're using non-blaming language. If your tone telegraphs judgment and disapproval, all the right words in the world will still make the person feel blamed and become defensive.

Use Humor to Take the Edge Off Your Message

Darlene is a director who works in the middle of a highly political, power-based leadership team.

"I don't know how she does it," says one of the VPs. "It's uncanny how she gets our attention and persuades us to do the right thing for our people. She has saved our bacon many times. She frames issues humorously. It makes her come across as completely non-confrontational. She somehow does it in a way that makes it feel like we're not losing face. It's pretty easy to say yes to her requests."

I've seen Darlene work her magic. She not only uses humor, but she also delivers her messages with a warm, authentic smile. This sends a clear signal that she bears no threat to her recipients.

However, here's an important caveat that a friend shared with us. "If someone is not accustomed to using humor in their regular communication, it can be dangerous to use it in a business setting. They may come off sounding sarcastic or like a smart aleck."

The learning here is: Find ways to use humor that are authentic for you.

Next time you need to pull a customer into your reality, lighten up. Use a smile and a bit of humor. That will do a better job of inviting them into your world than a frowning face and menacing message.

What Are We Really Saying Here?

- The face-to-face element of directness makes your message more contagious, produces feelings of trust, and sends clear meaning-making signals to your listener.

- Being direct earns you people's respect.

- Speaking your truth directly = being more productive.

- When being direct, be sure to use non-blaming language and humor.

Put the Sticking Point to Work

Focus on face-to-face sales calls this week rather than phoning and e-mailing. Pay attention to the impact you have on your customers as you let your chemistry go to work for you.

Chapter 11

IT'S A TWO-WAY STREET
Checking Your Customer's Understanding

The two chapters previous to this covered the steps of inviting customers into your world and helping them see your reality. But there's a crucial third step.

Help Them Reflect Back What They've Understood

When you've pulled others into your reality, it's crucial for you to check their understanding of what you've been saying.

Intelligent people often fall prey to this dynamic: "I'm sure I understand. Let's move on!" Meanwhile, they haven't fully grasped the essence of what the speaker was trying to convey. When your customers are pressuring you to move on, it may be important to ensure that they're on track with you.

This lesson came through to us with force in our work with

the commercial leadership team of a pharmaceutical organization. "Reg," the VP of sales, had returned from a dynamic training intervention. He shared a short, passionate message about what had happened to him and how it was going to change things for the team.

When Reg had finished speaking, we asked him to ask every member of the team to reflect back what they had heard. After each one had done so, we asked Reg to let each one know whether he felt they had understood him or not.

It was stunning to see eight very bright individuals not be able to accurately reflect back the essence of Reg's short, passionate message.

This closing-the-loop exercise produced a significant effect: The team members were able to see and feel Reg's reality, and this contributed to a breakthrough of cohesiveness and unity.

Effective Ways to Prevent Misunderstandings

How much connection do you leave on the table when you don't close the loop? How much misunderstanding or missed understanding do you have to go back and repair because you don't take the time to ask people to reflect back what they've heard?

Consider what Loretta A. Malandro says about this in her book *Say It Right the First Time*[*]:

> You will spend ten times the mental energy recovering from a misunderstanding than you would have spent preventing it.

---

[*] Loretta A. Malandro, *Say It Right the First Time* (New York: McGraw-Hill Professional, 2003).

There are effective and ineffective ways to do this. Avoid these ineffective ways:

• "Do you understand?"

• "Do you know what I mean?"

• "Am I making sense?"

Ninety percent of the time you will receive the same answer to all three of these questions: "Yes." This gives you little indication whether the person has truly understood you or not.

Here are some more effective ways to check someone's understanding:

• "Can I ask you to reflect this back to me so you and I can be sure we're on the same page?"

• "How does that sound to you?"

• "What are the implications of this for you?"

These questions are more likely to elicit a response that will give you a window into how accurate the person's understanding is.

Note the third question in particular. The implication question is one of the most effective ways to check someone's understanding. If they can tell you the implications of your message (rather than simply repeating back your words), there is a very good chance that they have completely understood your intent.

What Are We Really Saying Here?

- Asking people to reflect back their understanding will help you prevent costly misunderstandings.

- Just as trust = speed, taking the time to check your understanding will save you a lot of time.

Put the Sticking Point to Work

In your next several sales calls, look for opportunities to check your customers' understanding by asking them to reflect back your message.

Chapter 12

PULL OUT THE BIGGER REALITY

Performing the Magic of 1 + 1 = 5

You may be thinking, "Pull Conversation is just active listening on steroids" or, "Isn't this really just *Getting to Yes* or some other kind of negotiation program?"

Both of these concepts are great, but neither captures the amazing magic that occurs when the Bigger Reality is pulled to the surface.

You already know how the whole is often greater than the sum of its parts. You know how your one unit of effort added to my one unit of effort can magically create five units of results.

What's astonishing, though, is the regularity with which you can achieve this magic with something as simple and commonplace as Pull Conversations. Why? Because these conversations are *the focusing mechanism that enables you to see the Bigger Reality*.

Let's turn our attention to the process of pulling out the Bigger Reality so you can more regularly enjoy the benefits of 1 + 1 = 5 in your relationships.

What's Important to You?

A construction company wanted to develop a portion of Toronto's shoreline. Construction relationships with the Toronto Region Conservation Authority had historically been problematic because of the inherent tension between economic progress and its impact on the environment.

Tension can be an amazing ally. There's something latent in it that can drive surprising results. It's called energy.

The question is, do you commonly release intelligent or destructive energy out of your business tension? Pull is what makes the difference.

In the past, the developers had pushed "economic growth for the city" and TRCA had pushed "negative ecological impact." But something was different this time around.

- The developers went in asking, "What's most important for you in this situation?" TRCA responded with its concerns about shoreline aesthetics, the health of Lake Ontario's underwater species, and the perception of Toronto's citizens.

- TRCA then reciprocated with, "What's most important for you?" The developers shared their concerns about unreasonable demands and how they impacted the speed, productivity, and profitability of the project.

Then the two groups did some good work in finding common ground. "What is it we both want here?" they asked. Here's what they discovered:

- "We both want a development that is aesthetically pleasing to Toronto's citizens."
- "We both want to take care of the environment."

When they identified common ground, a great idea emerged: "What if we build extended underwater shoals to expand Toronto's fish habitat?"

This Bigger Reality energized both TRCA and the developers and paved the way for a productive and ecologically friendly solution.

The point of this story is simple: *Pulling out the Bigger Reality in any situation releases intelligent energy from the business tension. Uncovering the Bigger Reality with your customers makes the smartest decisions become apparent and unlocks the best results.*

In this chapter you will learn the two critical steps involved in pulling out the Bigger Reality:

Step 1:
Bring your two worlds together to find common ground.

Step 2:
Draw out the assumptions that obscure the Bigger Reality.

How to Bring Your Worlds Together to Find Common Ground

One linguistic device and one question will equip you to stand in the middle of business tension with your customer and bring your two worlds together to find common ground:

- The linguistic device: The word *and*, used the right way, has the effect of joining your worlds together.

- The question: Ask, "What is it we both want here?"

Join Your Worlds Together with "And"
Our language often broadcasts our intentions.

Try this experiment. Consider how it would go if you said to a customer:

> I know you feel it's important to flip the switch on the new technology immediately, *but* I think we need to spend more time preparing your employees for this change.

This formulation may send a signal to your customer that you have scant intentions of seeking to find the common ground between your world and theirs. They see you as having an *either/or* mindset versus an *and* mindset.

The word *but* is a powerful wedge that drives our two worlds apart and enhances the tension between us.

In fact, I've heard of research that suggests that when you join two statements together with the word *but*, over 90% of

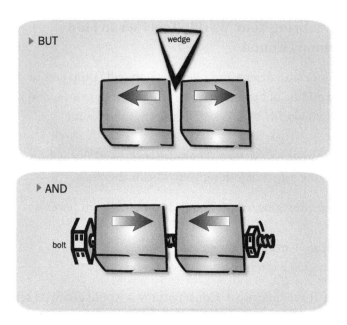

listeners cannot remember the first statement — they become fixated on the second.

For example, consider what happens when a husband says, "I love you honey, *but* ..." Whatever follows the word *but* shoulders out the *I love you*.

Or what happens when someone says, "The quality of your work is excellent, *but* I need you to increase your output"? All that sticks in the hearer's memory is, "You're not giving me enough output." The word *but* has summarily eradicated strength and highlighted deficiency.

In contrast, the word *and* can be a powerful little tool to join your worlds together.

For example, in terms of the story above about the technology launch, the wording could be, "I know you feel it's important to flip the switch on the new technology immediately, *and* I think we need to ensure that your employees are fully prepared for this change. Is there a way for both of us to achieve our goals?"

Ask, *"What Is It We Both Want Here?"*

Melissa is a pharmaceutical rep who calls on orthopedic surgeons. Her goal is to help make their practices successful by creating value — as defined by them. To create this value, she must build a relationship with the surgeons.

The surgeons, however, have no time for relationships. Melissa constantly hears the refrain, "I have no time to see you. I'm on my way to the elevator. I can give you three minutes."

She knows she has a drug that can help a surgeon's practice, but she can't get him to give her enough time to explain its benefits.

So she decides to try a different approach: a blend of directness and inquiry that gets both parties to common ground.

"I need just two minutes of your time, Dr. Naylor," she says.

What can she accomplish in two minutes? Melissa is going to try to quickly identify the common ground that will enable her to move the relationship forward.

"I want to be very respectful of your time and the busyness of your schedule. May I be direct with you?"

"Of course."

"What is it we both want here? Is there some common ground that would give both of us value?"

"I don't know if there is something we both want. You want me to spend time with you. I need to spend time with my end-stage and critical-care patients."

"Yes, that's true. But I think I see something else that we both want."

"What's that?"

"We both want more operating room time for you and less time spent in activities that don't add value to your practice. Would that be accurate?"

"It certainly would."

"I have enabled other surgeons to do exactly that."

"How?"

"It's about the way our drug is applied. The first injection of our pain-relief drug is applied by you, but the two subsequent injections can be given at an injection clinic. The patient is just as happy and your time is freed up."

"I can see that will give me more time in the O.R., but how else will it help my practice?"

"It creates a relationship with the injection clinic that gives them an added revenue stream. They respond by sending you more referrals."

"That makes sense."

"For me to walk you through how this can drug can work for you, I need an uninterrupted sixty minutes of your time. You probably need to eat sometime during the day. If you're interested, I'll bring in some sushi and we can talk over lunch. Would that work for you?"

"If you can keep my patients happy and give me more time in the O.R., of course it would."

"Then I'll set up a time with your office manager?"

"Yes, go ahead and do that."

Finding out "what is it we both want?" has two aspects to it:

• Discovering the things you want that are different from what I want (both of our unique needs).

• Discovering the things that we both want together (our common ground).

When Melissa enabled the surgeon to see that there was common ground between them (maximizing operating room time), it was a relatively easy step to uncover a Bigger Reality (the injection clinic) that would add value to the surgeon's practice and increase the number of scripts she generated within that practice.

This is performing the magic of $1 + 1 = 5$.

We have discovered that one of the best ways to uncover the common ground that will release energy from a stuck situation is to ask, "What is it we both want here?"

Avoid "Dichotomy Thinking"
People usually don't ask this question, however. Most often, the conversation fixates on what it is we *don't want.* Opposition

triggers a fear of either losing something you have or not getting something you want.

When this happens, a common reaction is to cut the issue in two, securing for yourself what you want and relinquishing to the other person what you can bear to live without. This *cutting up of the issue* produces a dichotomy (which means, literally, "to cut in two"), which makes it almost impossible to get to the Bigger Reality.

Dichotomy thinking cuts issues in half that, if left whole, would drive us to discover common ground. Common ground thinking creates a more fruitful outcome, giving us more of what we both want.

In their book *Getting to Yes,*＊ Fisher, Ury, and Patton describe two children quarreling over an orange. Their solution is to cut it in two. One eats the meat and throws the peel away. The other uses the peel of her half for baking a cake and throws the meat away.

Dichotomy thinking gave both of them half of what they wanted when each could have had the whole of what they wanted.

Common ground can't start on the basis of a dichotomy. Why? Because there's a real possibility that "what we both want together" will be something different from what can be envisioned from either point of view in the dichotomy. If *that* picture were to be filled in, it's very possible the result would be something different from what either "side" is currently imagining.

＊　Roger Fisher, William L. Ury, and Bruce Patton, *Getting to Yes*, second edition (New York: Penguin Books, 1991).

Give this a try. Ask, "What is it we both want here?" In essence, this simple question shifts your focus from defensiveness and protectionism to opportunity and possibility. It opens the way to discover the intersection between your needs and the needs of the customer. It reveals a piece of common ground you can both stand on and build on.

Draw Out the Assumptions That Obscure the Bigger Reality

I'm trying to get everybody to listen to the CBC: the Conversation Beside the Conversation. When you engage with a customer, there is a spoken conversation and another, unspoken conversation happening beside it in their head. What's happening in their head is the CBC.

The CBC is where the real decisions get made. It's the executive decision center. The customer may say, "I'll need a bit of time to talk to some of my colleagues and think this over," but the CBC is, "There's no way I could justify this kind of pricing."

The CBC eats the spoken conversation's lunch every day. The CBC is where the customer's assumption and belief tapes are rolling. Why is the CBC so powerful? Because beliefs drive behaviors every time.

Here's where *pull* can help you. As you step into your customer's world and seek to see and feel their reality (their CBC), you begin to straightforwardly inquire into the mental models that govern their decision making. In essence, you begin to engage that little voice inside their head.

You might say, "There are usually one or two aspects of our approach that certain customers are not comfortable with. What might those be for you?"

Your goal is to tune into CBC, the conversation beside the conversation, so you can draw out sticking points and core emotional needs.

But just as importantly, you need to broadcast your own CBC to the customer. Perhaps the customer has let you know about a tight timeline and has shown interest in your product yet is putting roadblocks in your way.

Don't allow these concerning thoughts and emotions to go unspoken. Use the blend of directness and inquiry to ask, "I'm a little confused. You indicated that you have a pressing deadline to make a decision and you seem to be interested in our solution. Yet you've just said that we can't get time with the ultimate decision maker. Can you help me reconcile these things?"

Remember this: To the extent that an unspoken conversation is playing in your head or your customer's, it is creating a lack of realism that will keep trust from *clicking* in the relationship. Tuning into the CBC is just another way of being "emotionally intelligent."

The Emotionally Intelligent Sales Rep
In the example of the sales rep and the surgeon, the rep could have easily been triggered when she showed up for a scheduled appointment and Dr. Naylor said, "I have no time to see you — I can give you three minutes."

Let us offer you Emotional Intelligence (EI) in capsule form.

- The first aspect of EI is the ability to be aware of your own emotional state and manage it through tough situations.

- The second is the ability to detect another's emotional state (without having to be told what it is).

- The third is to then help them manage through tough situations.

If you fail at self-awareness or other-awareness, good luck navigating any tough emotional waters.

Why is this a critical learning? Consider the following example.

Steve is a pet food sales rep who calls on veterinarians. He is attempting to win some shelf space in an animal hospital. The vet begins to push back with a few sarcastic objections about how much corn-filler is contained in Steve's product.

Steve can feel his anger start to rise up. He begins to lose his ability to manage his emotions. He starts arguing with the vet about corn, spouting research, statistics, and studies.

Thankfully, his manager, Yvonne, is with him on this call.

- She steps in and begins pulling. "It feels like we may be getting off track here."

- Bringing out her understanding of the vet's CBC, she says, "When you look at the prospect of us asking you for shelf space that is currently occupied by our competitor, what are the most important concerns that come to your mind?"

• "Well, the science they give us is amazing," comes the response. "They provide very valuable continuing education events for my staff. But most importantly, they continue to demonstrate a support for our profession that few of you other providers demonstrate. I think that's what's most important to me."

Where did his concern about corn-filler go? It's not even on his radar screen. Yvonne pulled and found that the shelf space issue was attached to something much more substantial: emotional and professional support.

This vet is making his decisions based on *conscience*. He would feel disloyal giving a competitor shelf space when he adds up all the strong expressions of support he has been offered by his current supplier.

If Steve is unable to detect this vet's emotional state (loyalty based on conscience), he will never be able to move this account forward.

Yvonne manages her emotions, uses the sticking point to pull out the emotional energizer, and begins to ask the vet about what support looks like inside his world. If she continues with this approach, she is very likely to craft a solution that will satisfy his definition for support.

How You Get Triggered

There is a physiological explanation for what happens to you when you react like Steve.

Your brain is made up of three main parts. The first is the brainstem. It is important only for those who want to have reflexes and a pulse — it regulates those autonomic functions.

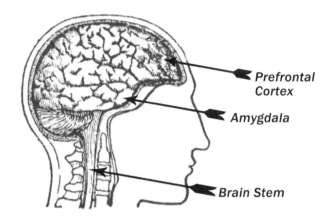

The second part of your brain is called the prefrontal cortex. It is responsible for all the rational decision making and information processing. The cortex acts like your CPU (central processing unit).

The third part of your brain is called the amygdala. It is a small, almond-shaped organ that acts like an emotional computer chip. It takes in and becomes deeply embedded with all of your emotional memories, highlighting the ones that will be instrumental to your safety.

Unless you grew up in an emotional vacuum, your amygdala has probably been encoded with a few emotional experiences that leave you open to being hijacked.

The Amygdala Hijack

What do you think of when you hear the word *hijack*? Probably something like *a sudden, violent loss of control.* This is the perfect description of what happens when your amygdala picks up a signal in the midst of a conversation that you're being threatened.

The interesting thing about the amygdala is that it can't tell the difference between a real or imagined event. When a stimulus enters the amygdala that resembles a past traumatic experience, the amygdala *assumes* that you're in the exact same situation. It secretes hormones into your body to prepare you for fight or flight. Cortisol is pumped into your prefrontal cortex, your sensory acuity is heightened, and your large muscles are prepared for action.

This response is brilliant in helping you wrestle or run from a saber-tooth tiger, but not so good in helping you with a tough conversation with a colleague. Why? Because when cortisol is pumped into your prefrontal cortex, your logical processing faculties are dramatically reduced.

Perhaps you've had times when you looked back on an argument and thought, "Why didn't I think of saying *x*? It would have been perfect." The reason is that you were literally stupid in the moment. You were the victim of a sudden, violent loss of control — an amygdala hijack.

But here's some good news. If you can recognize that you're being hijacked, you can flush the cortisol out of your prefrontal cortex and regain your logic. Cortisol is flushed out by three things: oxygen, time, and gratitude. Here are three steps to take the next time you recognize your body gearing up and your mind shutting down:

Step 1: *Oxygenate*. (The old adage of taking ten deep breaths is valid.)

Step 2: Ask for some *time*. ("Can we take break and then come back to this?")

Step 3: Lock into and visualize an incident in which you were particularly **grateful**. (For me, this was the moment in a phone call in which I learned that my son Tyler had escaped unharmed from a rolled vehicle that had burst into flames.) Gratitude sends a wash of hormones — dopamine, serotonin, endorphins — that flush the cortisol out of your body.

Focused Attention Increases Performance
Here's another mechanism that can help you stay focused when a customer starts to dig in and resist you: focused attention. This technique was pioneered by Timothy Gallwey and Allen Fine. They learned from the discipline of sports psychology that when an athlete focuses his attention on the critical variables of his game, it removes interference and improves performance.

In tennis, the critical variables are the ball, the net, the lines on the court, and the position of the opponent.

In the sales game, the critical variables are *interest* and *ease*.

Corporate athletes can learn to remove the interference associated with customer resistance by focusing on these two critical variables.

Try it. Next time you're speaking to a customer, focus on her interest level. Calibrate it from 1 to 10, with 1 being, "She is absolutely not interested in what I have to say" and 10 being, "She is completely interested in what I have to say."

As you focus your attention on the customer's interest level, it will reduce your interference and your mind and body will begin to perform at a higher level, doing the things that will secure a more productive outcome in the conversation.

When the customer is speaking, focus your attention on the level of ease you notice in her face, voice, and body language. Calibrate it from 1 to 10, with 1 being, "She is absolutely not at ease" and 10 being, "She is completely at ease." Read Gallwey's book *The Inner Game of Work* to more fully understand the fascinating science behind this.

What Are We Really Saying Here?

+ Pull is the focusing mechanism that enables you to see the Bigger Reality.

+ "And" can be a powerful little tool for joining your worlds together.

+ Ask, "What is it we both want here?" to uncover the common ground that will release energy in a stuck situation.

+ When faced with resistance, use your emotional intelligence to tune into what's happening under the surface, at the emotional level.

+ When you recognize that you're having an amygdala hijack, oxygenate, ask for time, and be grateful for the other person's reality.

+ Focus your attention on your customer's interest and ease to remove the emotional interference associated with a customer digging in or attacking you.

Put the Sticking Point to Work

This week, use the focusing techniques from this chapter with your customers. When you're speaking, focus on and calibrate your customer's level of interest. When your customer is speaking, focus on and calibrate their level of ease.

Chapter 13

PULL OUT PEOPLE'S BEST STUFF

Releasing Brilliance Through Respect

I love the story of the man who had dealings with two British prime ministers, William Gladstone and Benjamin Disraeli. "Whenever I came away from a conversation with [Gladstone]," he said, "I was left with the feeling of how brilliant he was. Whenever I came away from a conversation with Benjamin Disraeli, I was left with the feeling of how brilliant *I* was."

Disraeli probably earned the right, then, to quip that "the greatest good you can do for another is not just to share your riches, but to reveal to him his own."

We have explored how Pull Conversations uncover the sticking point that leads you to your customer's core emotional need. Meet this need and you engage your customer. Everything we have said so far is predicated on one crucial heart-set: respect.

Respect

There's a scene in the movie *Erin Brokovich* that I'm particularly fond of. Brokovich is at an impasse. She needs that one critical piece of evidence, that "smoking gun" that will solve the case. It is nowhere to be found until, like a magnet, she attracts it directly to herself.

Why did the plant worker offer her the case-winning tip? My theory is that the respect Erin demonstrated to this man energized him to help her succeed. Her first instinct was to pull away from him. She got past herself, took a second look at the man, and decided to have a conversation with him.

Interestingly enough, having another look is exactly what respect is all about. It comes from a Latin word *respecere*, which means, "to look again." William Isaacs, in his book *Dialogue: The Art of Thinking Together,*° says that respect "involves a sense of honoring or deferring to someone. Where once we saw one aspect of a person, we look again and realize how much of them we had missed."

The essence of respect, then, is *to look again to recognize someone's true potential and to treat them accordingly.*

What impact will this have on your customers?

Respect Facilitates Learning

I noticed something early in my career that I later came to call "blinds down." When people who were teaching me a procedure

---

° William Isaacs, *Dialogue: The Art of Thinking Together* (New York: Doubleday Currency, 1999).

were abrupt, impatient, or patronizing, I would begin to stumble over my words and my thoughts. It was almost as if the blinds would go down over my eyes. There I was, a bumbling idiot who couldn't offer what was inside me to give.

As I double-checked myself, however, I came to see that the problem wasn't my intelligence or lack of it.

I knew that I was eager to learn and willing to understand.

I could see that other people were having the same difficulty with the same "teachers."

And I felt articulate and bright when I was around people who took me through the same learning process but demonstrated that they valued my thoughts. I ended up being able to understand in half the time.

The difference between these two types of teachers was simple. The first showed me no respect. The second did. The raw material that was available to each was precisely the same: my best stuff. One type forfeited it and the other got it all.

I've had participants by the thousands confirm this phenomenon, telling me that the key trait releasing their intelligence and efforts may be said in different ways but it all spells R-E-S-P-E-C-T:

- "He makes me feel valued."

- "She genuinely listens to me."

- "He gives me his undivided attention."

- "He is nonjudgmental."

- "She asks great questions."

If you need your customer to be engaged with you in order to uncover the best solution for them, you will need all their energy and all their intelligence. Here's your choicepoint: If you want to work with brilliant customers, it's your respect for them that will draw out their brilliance. And as we will see, how you treat customers is predicated on how you see them.

Person or Thing?

I drive a Saturn. It runs well and gets great mileage. I'll probably keep it. But if it starts to burn oil or give me transmission problems, I will get rid of it. Why? Because my Saturn is just a tool — a thing. I value and respect it only for its utility to me. I have no emotional attachment to it whatsoever.

There are two ways to look at people: as tools or as human beings. If, over time, you have begun to value people only for what they can do for you, then you've lost your ability to see them as human beings. You're seeing them only as tools to get a certain result.

If this is your M.O., no number of Pull Conversations will humanize your sales approach.

If They Don't Feel It, It's Not There

But it's not enough to respect your customer; they must *feel respected* by you.

Unfortunately, the skill of closing the feeling loop to make sure people feel respected is often missed by those who have a high IQ but an underdeveloped EQ (emotional quotient).

Jerry is a new employee speaking to his boss, Raj. Jerry is processing through point A, point B, and point C. Raj has already gone from point A to K — he's got a clear understanding of the issue and knows where Jerry is going to end up. He starts telling Jerry, "I've got it. I've *got* it. You don't have to tell me any more."

But Jerry feels he needs to process points D, E, F, G, H, I, J, and K to feel that he is perfectly clear in his own thinking.

Now he feels disrespected.

In his book *Working with Emotional Intelligence,*[*] Daniel Goleman discusses scientific evidence of the physical effects on people when they are disrespected or respected.

Goleman says that when we experience stress — for example, when we're being psychologically "erased" or simply ignored by others — our bodies release cortisol, sometimes called the stress hormone. Among other things, cortisol is intimately connected to the functioning of the immune system. That's why stressful situations affect our physical well-being.

He points out that, by contrast, when we're positively engaged, "our brain is being soaked in a bath of catecholamines and other substances triggered by the adrenal system. These chemicals prime the brain to stay attentive and interested, even fascinated, and energized for a sustained effort."

Goleman describes the kind of listening that draws out brilliance as simply "being present." When people are present for us, it sets off these positive reactions in our very being. It's easy

---

[*] Daniel Goleman, *Working with Emotional Intelligence* (New York: Bantam Books, 1998).

to see why brilliance is much more likely to be displayed when people experience truly positive regard.

Respect Unlocks Your Customers' Discretionary Effort

Many years ago I developed an exercise to show participants exactly what is withheld from someone who does not respect others. This exercise also demonstrates *why* people withhold their discretionary effort. After polling thousands of participants, I grew confident that the data emerging from this exercise were highly accurate.

In the exercise, I asked participants to think of the best listener they had ever known, someone who made them feel respected. I asked them, "What are the things this person does as a listener that make you feel respected?"

They came back with:

* "They give me their undivided attention."

* "They're genuine."

* "They don't interrupt me."

* "They acknowledge what I say with nods and facial expressions."

* "They're nonjudgmental."

* "They reflect back what I say to be sure they understand."

Then I gave them a stack of cards representing all the valuable resources inside them, such as vision, innovations, constructive feedback, and tried-and-true techniques.

"Which of these things would you offer to your best listener, the person who makes you feel respected?" I asked.

"All of them."

"Now think about your worst listener, someone who does not make you feel respected and understood. What types of things do they do?"

Their list:

- "They interrupt me."
- "They're judgmental and jump to conclusions."
- "They don't give good eye contact."
- "They monopolize the conversation."
- "They only act like they're listening."
- "They answer phone calls in the middle of what I'm saying."
- "They finish my sentences for me."

My next question: "What would you freely offer a person like this and what would you not offer them?"

They said they would offer four basics:

- Basic information.
- Accurate instructions.
- Warnings.
- Tried-and-true techniques.

The majority said that they would withhold all their other resources. This means that people who make others feel disrespected forfeit such critical resources as vision, innovation, misgivings, constructive feedback, respect, empathy, enthusiasm, encouragement, and loyalty.

"Now let's think about someone who makes you feel moderately respected and understood," I said. "What will you offer them?"

They listed off their innovations, tried-and-true techniques, constructive feedback, misgivings, and encouragement.

"What resources is this person still missing out on?" I asked next.

"They don't get our vision, respect, loyalty, empathy, or enthusiasm. They don't get those things until they make us feel *completely* respected and understood."

Are You Missing Out on Your Customers' Best Stuff?

Are you guilty of any of the misdemeanors on the Worst Listener list? Are you oblivious to the idiosyncrasies that you're exhibiting? If so, people may only feel moderately respected and understood by you. Our research shows that if this is true, you're probably forfeiting their vision, respect, loyalty, empathy, and enthusiasm.

Think of the implications of this. If they're not offering you these resources, do you think they're offering you their trust? Likely not. Think of the further implications. Take a close look at the resources that they're withholding. Do you notice anything about them? They represent the deepest part of the person, the part that juices and energizes them.

The tragedy in all this is that most people *want* to offer you their best stuff. Relatively few are spitefully holding back their resources from you.

Disrespect and misunderstanding have an impact not only on people's *willingness*. More significantly, they also have an impact on people's *ability* to offer you their best stuff.

How to Show Respect

If you want to really see people's potential, it's quite possible that you will need to learn how to respect or "look again."

Here are twenty-one behaviors that you can demonstrate in order to make people feel respected and understood.

1. Learn what kind of eye contact makes them comfortable with you.

2. Use body language that opens them up.

3. Give them your undivided focus, and vigilantly protect the conversation from distractions.

4. Don't jump to conclusions or give in to the urge to judge.

5. Don't finish their sentences for them. Leave generous listening spaces.

6. Acknowledge them with your body and your voice.

7. Reflect back the essence of their message to demonstrate that you understand their viewpoint.

8. Don't dismiss their ideas, but "look again" until you find the validity in them.

9. Eliminate any patronizing or condescending tones.

10. Challenge their thinking in respectful ways.

11. Show patience while they process.

12. Be inquisitive about what's important to them.

13. Remember and quote things they've said in prior conversations.

14. Listen intently to discover what's going on beneath the surface of the conversation.

15. Use appropriate follow-up as an exclamation point to demonstrate that you understand and respect what they said.

16. Only ask for people's input authentically — that is, if you're truly open to being changed by what they offer.

17. Step into their world and see the issue the way they see it.

18. Look for the potential in them that others do not recognize.

19. Demonstrate confidence that they're able to understand you.

20. Understand their point of view before trying to make them understand yours.

21. Hear not only what they're saying but also what they're trying to say.

Caveat

True respect cannot be manufactured. It's something that oozes out of you. Others know that it's there — or not.

When you respect someone, they walk away from you with something wonderful sticking to them.

If you're coming to the conclusion that you do not respect people, do some heart-searching. Ask yourself, "Why doesn't respect ooze out of me?"

Respect Is Person-Specific

Are the skills of respect person-specific or universal?

Certain things leave one person feeling respected and another disrespected. Eye contact and body language are like that. The eye contact I use to make an orthodox Jewish woman feel respected would leave an Arab man feeling insulted. The body language I use with my friend Alex would leave my friend Rick feeling claustrophobic.

How can you know for sure whether you're making people feel respected and understood? Become an astute student of every person you converse with. Here is where stepping into other people's worlds is so critical to your success. It gives you the relational radar to know what's appropriate in each situation.

The best measure to use is the quality and depth of the data that people are offering you. If you see someone starting to close off, it's time to alter your approach.

Manage These Eight Deadly Distractions

1. Scripting while you listen: "Hmmm. What do I want to say next?"

2. Future worry churn: "I better make sure I don't forget to pick up the kids."

3. Past regret churn: "I shouldn't have yelled at the CEO this morning."

4. Present churn: "Oh no, I need to get at that proposal!"

5. Spiritual churn: "I am *way* off-center today."

6. Interruptions: phone calls, BlackBerry messages, people walking in, people walking out.

7. Biological needs: fatigue, hunger, hotness, coldness, full bladder.

8. Environmental noise: TV, music, machinery, kids.

What Are We Really Saying Here?

• The essence of respect is to look again in order to recognize someone's true potential and treat them accordingly.

• If, over time, you have come to value people only for what they can do for you, then you've lost your ability to see them as persons and you're seeing them as things.

- You can surround yourself with bright people; make sure you give them the respect that draws out their brilliance.

- Your respect is of little worth to someone unless they feel it. Your job is to communicate it in such a way that they can do so.

- One of the best ways to show someone that you respect them is to reflect back the essence of what they're saying. This shows that you value their viewpoint.

- People withhold their richest inner resources from those who don't make them feel completely respected.

- Respect can't be manufactured. It has to simply ooze out of you.

Put the Sticking Point to Work

Pick the distraction you most need to work on from the Eight Deadly Distractions list above. This week, pay attention to your progress in managing this one distraction.

Chapter 14

THE PULL CONVERSATION SALES APPROACH

Engaging Your Customers

To engage a customer, you must perform the usual four phases of the sales process:

- The rehearsal.
- The sales call.
- The debrief.
- The follow-up.

The Rehearsal

Professional athletes and professional musicians know something that we professional business people have forgotten: the power of rehearsing.

CUSTOMER ENGAGEMENT WORKSHEET

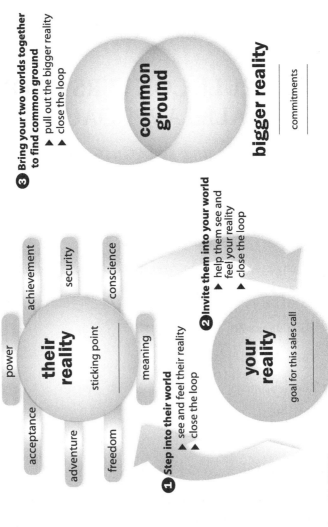

power achievement security

their reality

sticking point

acceptance

adventure freedom meaning conscience

1 **Step into their world**
▲ see and feel their reality
▲ close the loop

2 **Invite them into your world**
▲ help them see and feel your reality
▲ close the loop

your reality

goal for this sales call

3 **Bring your two worlds together to find common ground**
▲ pull out the bigger reality
▲ close the loop

common ground

bigger reality

commitments

Can you imagine a professional athlete showing up for an event without having practiced? Can you imagine a professional musician showing up for a concert without having rehearsed?

Yet salespeople show up for important sales calls thinking, "It will come to me in the moment." No wonder business gets left on the table.

So the first part of the Pull Conversation sales approach begins with rehearsal. Skim through your profile notes. What has transpired in this account to date? Have you delivered on everything you've promised? Are there any important birthday or anniversary events your client is celebrating?

If it's a new prospect, step into their world and learn all you can about them: their history, their values, who they've dealt with in the past, etc.

Research Their World
Write your notes around the **Their Reality** world on the Customer Engagement Worksheet.

Write Down Your Goal
Then identify the goal you want to achieve on this call and write it on the **Your Reality** world on the worksheet. Some examples could be:

◆ Meet to determine whether there could be a fit.

◆ Gain a clear picture of the customer's needs.

◆ Discover who the decision makers are and what their criteria are for buying.

◆ Book a meeting with the decision makers.

- Present the proposal to create clear understanding about the value we bring.

- Close the sale.

- Check progress to ensure that the customer is delighted.

- Ask for referrals.

Anticipate Possible Sticking Points

In the world entitled **Their Reality**, list the possible sticking points you might encounter on this sales call. A few examples could be:

- Loyalty to current provider.

- Quality concerns.

- No time.

- Price sensitivity.

- Compatibility concerns.

Identify Emotional Energizers

If you have a previous history with this customer, circle the top three energizers that they will refuse to do without. Which three are most important to them?

- Power.

- Achievement.

- Security.

- Conscience.

- Meaning.

- Freedom.

- Adventure.

- Acceptance.

Identify the Common Ground
What is the common ground between what is most important to you and what is most important to your customer? Ask yourself, "What is it we both want here?" Write it under **Common Ground**.

Bigger Reality and Commitments
Leave these categories empty for now. You will fill them out after the sales call is complete.

The Sales Call

We have dealt with how to do the sales call at length in this book. Here is the sales call process in a nutshell.

1. Step into their world.

   - See and feel their reality.

   - Reflect it back in your own words.

2. Invite them into your world.

   - Help them see your reality.

   - Help them reflect it back.

3. Bring your two worlds together to find common ground.

    * Pull out the Bigger Reality.

    * Summarize your commitments.

Note: When you invite your customer into your world and begin to help them see what's important to you, their sticking point will typically emerge (in relation to price, delivery, functionality, access, etc.). When it does, go back to step one to pull out the emotional energizer attached to their sticking point. Then frame your solution in a way that helps them see a clear picture in which you are meeting that need.

The Debrief

After you've left the sales call, revisit:

* The Sticking Points and Emotional Energizers

    * What sticking points (if any) emerged in this call?

    * What emotional energizers became apparent?

    * Make notes in or around the **Their Reality** world.

* Your Goal

    * Did you achieve your goal for the call?

    * If not, what is the reformulated goal for your next meeting?

* The Common Ground

    * What emerged as the common ground from your conversation?

- The Bigger Reality

  - What was the **Bigger Reality** — the surprising solution that gave both of you what you wanted?

  - Fill in the section beneath the **Common Ground** worlds.

- The Commitments

  - What commitments do you need to deliver on and in what time frames?

  - Who do you need to communicate with to fulfill these commitments?

  - How will you close the loop with the client to demonstrate that you have delivered on their commitments?

  - What do you need to do to ensure that they deliver on their commitments?

The Follow-up

Perhaps you've engaged the customer to move to the next level. Now you're going to deliver on your commitments in a way that meets their core emotional energizers. For example:

- If their energizer is **adventure**, deliver your product or solution with an element of creativity and surprise.

- If their energizer is **security**, deliver your product or solution systematically and methodically.

- If their energizer is **freedom**, deliver in a way that demands as little of their time and thought as possible.

But perhaps they haven't moved to the next level and you still want to pursue them.

In such a case, your understanding of their core emotional energizers will inform your future approach: Every piece of communication you send them will highlight how you can increase the adventure, security, or freedom levels in their lives.

What Are We Really Saying Here?

- Pull Conversations deepen the normal four phases of the sales process: the rehearsal, the sales call, the debrief, and the follow-up.

- They bring into focus the strategy of aligning the customer's reality with what you offer.

Put the Sticking Point to Work

Use the worksheet on page 132 to rehearse for an important upcoming sales call. Fill in every relevant aspect of the worksheet and notice the difference this makes in the quality of your call.

CONCLUSION

What Are We Really Saying in This Book?

- You get the best results from your customers when they're juiced, energized, and engaged.

- Customer engagement happens naturally when their core emotional needs are being met.

- Your customer's core emotional needs are hidden beneath the surface, but they're attached by a string to their sticking point.

- When you *pull* with directness and inquiry, you're able to acknowledge the sticking point and draw out the core emotional need attached to it.

- When you find the common ground between your needs and the customer's needs, a Bigger Reality emerges: a solution that is more surprising and powerful than just win-win.

- This stuff works only when respect oozes out of you.

Thank you for reading this book. I would love to hear how you have put the Sticking Point Process to work. E-mail your story to me at bradywilson@juiceinc.com.

Cheers,
Brady

INDEX

amygdala, 20, 113–115
"and" or "but," 103–105
Asacker, Tom, 18, 20
assumptions, obscuring reality,
    109–116

Bachrach, Bill, 38
Bigger Reality, pulling out, 45,
    100–117, 140
    bringing two worlds together,
        102–109
    drawing out assumptions,
        109–112
    focused attention, 115–116
    managing emotions, 110–115
brain
    and emotional reactions, 20,
        112–114
    as open-loop system, 84–86
buying decisions

emotional energizers, 22–28,
    33–35, 61–63, 112
emotional needs and, 15, 17–21,
    26–28, 34, 52
first and last impressions, 20
relationships and (*see* relation-
    ship with customer)

CBC (Conversation Beside
    Conversation), 109–110, 111
change by seeing and feeling,
    73–75
Clarke, Boyd and Crossland, Ron, 77
common ground, finding, 59–64,
    102–109, 135, 136
conversation, *see* CBC; face-to-
    face conversation; pull
    conversation
customer engagement, 26, 27, 63,
    91, 131–138, 139

customer engagement work-
sheet, *132*
customer's world and your world,
5–6, 26–27, 34, 133–136
joining two worlds, 102–109,
132, 136
stepping into customer's world,
49–58, 69–72, 135
stepping out of your world,
54–57
welcoming customers to your
world, 73–80, 135

Deming, W. Edward, 36
Denning, Stephen, 77–79
"dichotomy thinking," avoiding,
107–109
directness, 41–42, 43, 44, 81–91
joining with inquiry, 45–48, 110,
112, 139
respect with, 88–90
speaking your truth productively,
91–95

emotional contagion, 83, 84–86
emotional energizers, 22–28,
134–135
meeting in follow-up, 137–138
uncovering, 24–28, 33–35, 49,
51, 61–63, 112, 136
Emotional Intelligence (EI),
110–115
emotional needs, 15, 18–19, 139
buying decisions and, 17–21,
26–28, 34, 52
uncovering (*see* emotional
energizers)
emotional states, 85, 111, 112
physiological explanation for,
112–114
regaining control of, 114–115

face-to-face conversation, 81–95
Fine, Allen, 115
first and last impressions, 20
focused attention, 115–116

Gallwey, Timothy, 115, 116
Getting to Yes (Fisher), 108
Goleman, Daniel, 83–84, 122

Hallowell, Edward M., 86–87
Heart of Change, The (Kotter),
73–75
humor, 94–95

Inner Game of Work, The
(Gallwey), 116
inquiry, 40–41, 42, 43, 44, 46–47
combining with directness,
45–48
invitational language, 73–80
inward focus of salespeople, 30–31

Johnson, Kerry L., 66
joining two worlds, 102–109
Juice Inc., 37

Khalsa, Mahan, 70
Knechtel, David, 1–2, 82
Kotter, John, 73–75

Leader's Voice, The (Clarke and
Crossland), 77
Let's Get Real or Let's Not Play
(Khalsa), 70
Letwin, Jim, 17
listening, 5, 16, 42
empathically, 67–69

and reflecting back, 65–72
with respect, 123–125

Malandro, Loretta A., 97
McCallum, Paul, 47
mental muscle memory (MMM),
    31–32, 33
mirror neurons, 83–84

narrative, *see* stories for communication
negative feelings, acknowledging,
    61–63
non-blaming language, 91–94
nonverbal cues, 68, 82, 87–88

open-loop system, brain as, 84–86

Primal Leadership (Goleman,
    others), 84–85
Pull Conversation, 1–2, 3, 9–16,
    29–30, 71, 76
    face-to-face, 81–95
    focusing mechanism, 100,
        115–116
    inquiry and directness, 40–48
        (*see also* directness; inquiry)
    reflecting customer's reality,
        65–67, 69 (*see also* reflecting
        back)
    sales process, *see* sales process
        and Pull Conversation
    uncovering emotional energizers,
        33–35
    use of stories and images, 76–80
        see also emotional energizers;
        listening
Pull Matrix, *43*
push or pull, 3
    example, 10–12

problem with push, 30
why most sales reps push,
    30–33, 54
why pulling works better, 12, 35,
    54

questions with empathy, 46–47,
    51, 68–69

reflecting back, 56, 65–72
    checking others' understanding,
        96–99
    empathic listening, 68–69
    showing respect, 126, 130
relationship tension and task
    tension, 52–54
relationship with customer, 9–10,
    13–14, 15, 16, 26–27
    interest of customer, *see*
        customer engagement
    trust, *see* trust *see also* customer's
        world and your world; joining
        two worlds
resistance to push, 30
respect, 119–130
    engaging customers, 119–121,
        122–126
    how to show respect, 126–128
    listening with, 123–125
    managing distractions, 129
    physical effects, 122
Risch, Karen, 38
Rohn, Jim, 41

Sales Magic (Johnson), 66
sales process and pull conversation
    debrief, 136–137
    follow-up, 137–138
    rehearsal, 131, 133–135
    sales call (summary), 135–136
sales style, 48

Social Intelligence (Goleman), 83–84
Speed of Trust, The (Covey), 36–37
sticking point
  anticipating, 134
  defined, 2
  emotional needs and, 19
  identifying, 13–15, 19, 35, 112, 136
  process, 4, 5–7
  see also emotional energizers; Pull Conversation; push or pull
stories for communication, 34, 76–80
symbols, 41, 77, 80

task tension, 53, 54
tension and energy, 101–102
Tournier, Paul, 38
trust
  emotional need and, 15
  importance, 9–10
  sales success and, 36–38, 44, 75

understanding and, 38, 54–57
  see also emotional needs
trust-building hormones, 86–87
truth
  combining goals (*see* Bigger Reality)
  speaking your truth productively, 91–95

understanding and trust, 38, 54–57
opportunities from conflicts, 59–64
reflecting a message, *see* reflecting back

Values-Based Selling (Bachrach and Risch), 38

Working with Emotional Intelligence (Goleman), 122

ALSO BY BRADY G. WILSON

- Volume discounts available on all three of Brady's books. Contact us for more details.

- Engage in conversation with us to discover meaningful, proven strategies for your organization, by calling 1-888-822-5479.

- Visit the Juice Resource Centre at www.juiceinc.com for information about upcoming workshops and speaking engagements, articles, and excerpts, and additional Juice resources, including The Juice Check™ — a tool designed to help you measure how much intelligent energy is released in your work environment.

- Brady Wilson is a highly animated, intensely pragmatic presenter, trainer, and consultant. He is a gifted keynote presenter on the topics of Communication, Employee Engagement, and Emotional Intelligence at Work.

For more information about Brady Wilson or Juice Inc.:

phone: 1-888-822-5479   e-mail: info@juiceinc.com

www.juiceinc.com

CPSIA information can be obtained at www.ICGtesting.com
Printed in the USA
LVOW011435280313

326529LV00008B/36/P